Dear Danuta:

I feel very strongly the importance of tithing. But my family needs my paycheck and my parents are against taking such a big chunk of money that could go to help out for food. I want to obey my parents. But I also want to uphold what is right with God.

———

Dear Danuta:

As a young woman, I am troubled by the attitude that a "good Christian woman should always be at home." You strike me as an independent, forceful woman. How do you feel about the choices Christian women are faced with nowadays? What *can* Christian women do?

———

Dear Danuta:

I need to change my life. Can you give me some advice about getting control of my diet, my finances, and my career?

———

Dear Danuta:

I don't know what to do about my son, who is nineteen years old. He has been going through real rebellion—drugs, profanity—and is completely out of control. He is also learning disabled, and has had a hard time in school.

———

Dear Danuta:

You're the one who "hooked" me on the show. You're not a saccharine, submissive, bubbleheaded bit of fluff, but a REAL WOMAN. You're so sure of your femininity that you feel free to do really fun things on the show, like panning for gold or using a bulldozer to level an outhouse.

Dear Danuta,

Dear Danuta,

Danuta Soderman

Fleming H. Revell Company
Old Tappan, New Jersey

Library of Congress Cataloging-in-Publication Data

Soderman, Danuta.
   Dear Danuta.

   1. Christian life—Miscellanea. 2. Conduct of life—Miscellanea. I. Title.
BV4510.2.S63   1986   248.4   86-538
ISBN 0-8007-1468-7

To
My
Beloved
Kai

Contents

Contents

Contents

Dear Reader,

As the co-host of the "700 Club" I receive thousands of letters a year from viewers. They come from all over the world, wherever the program reaches—a trailer park in Kansas, a fancy New Jersey suburb, the streets of Waikiki, the Philippines, Nigeria, even China! Some letters are scrawled on bits of paper, napkins, paper towels, some written in an elegant hand on personalized stationery, some written with a word processor, some on prison letterhead.

I try to read every letter and to answer each one personally: it's an almost impossible task, but one for which I feel tremendous responsibility. Each person who writes to me makes an effort to touch me. These people consider me a friend whom they have come to know from watching the "700 Club" each day. They have come to trust me and to confide some of their deepest pains and hopes. There have been many letters that have moved me to tears, made me howl with laughter or sigh with delight. They always keep me busy in prayer. If these dear people care enough to write to me, I am obligated to care enough to answer.

As one of the letter writers put it, "Danuta, you say that a career was possible for you because you have no children needing you. But my dear, you do have a multitude of children depending on you—your viewers!"

This "multitude of children" has continued to lay open its heart to me. People write about the loneliness of the single life, the despair of a lost job or a broken family, homosexuality, the pain of cancer, fear for a parent, husband, or child who has turned from God. The problems are different, but each letter sounds a similar note:

"Dear Danuta . . . help me. Tell me God hasn't forgotten me."
"Danuta, I have done so many things to make God angry. Speak to Him for me. Maybe He'll listen to you."

11

I find myself reminding people all the time that God does not just hear my prayers or the prayers of anybody on television because He gets cable up there ... but because we have a mediator in Jesus. Jesus didn't just die for Christian celebrities, but for any who call on His name. Their prayers are as effective as mine if they understand the power of the blood of Christ. Nothing is more basic to Christianity than the fact that Christ died for all of us. All our prayers are heard through Him.

Perhaps the greatest need of these letters is for encouragement. So many viewers need to know how to hang on, how to wait for God's plan to be revealed and even why to wait on Him!

Those who write to me seem to know that the Danuta on screen is not so different from the Danuta in private. I try not to mince words or dodge issues. And I believe that if you don't like your life, you can change it.

My viewers know what to expect from me—not necessarily agreement but sometimes pretty tough-minded advice always given in love. And so I write back: "Save the marriage ..." "Get off welfare." "Stop waiting for Mr. Right and make the other parts of your life meaningful so that you will be worthy to love." "Take action. You can unravel a cobweb strand by strand."

It is not that I have a corner on the market in wisdom. My practical advice is always undergirded by a Wisdom greater than my own—the Wisdom gained by trust in God's Word and in His Son, Jesus Christ.

As my mail continues to mount, so has my conviction that this correspondence is a vital part of my ministry. Through it, I have been blessed with an immediate pipeline to my viewers. And in themselves, the letters are moving and potent reminders that we are not alone in this world with our tragedies and secrets, our pains and problems. We have all been touched by suffering. The great wonder and comfort is that Christ knows and He listens; He cares and He lifts us up from hopelessness and despair.

Perhaps you will find a bit of yourself in these cries and whispers of searching hearts. Perhaps you will find a good word, a little encouragement, a kick in the pants, or maybe even a hug. My hope is that this collection of cries and whispers will speak to you as they always do to me—of the ongoing miracle of God's love for all of us.

With love,

What was your name again?

Dear Danuta:
I'm a "700 Club" member and watch the show every day—mostly.

I'm the one who forgot your lamb's name. So I wrote to you and you were so kind to respond by telling me it was Emma.

I've forgotten your name (last) before you married Mr. Soderman. Please humor an old lady, seventy-four years old, and answer me so I can think about something else. Tell me your last name before you married—I will thank you kindly.

P.S. I worry when I forget something.

[Before she married, Danuta's last name was Rylko.]

Part 1

"I feel like
such a failure . . ."

How can I stop hating myself?

So many times I get letters from people who really don't know how to accept themselves the way the good Lord made them. Self-esteem runs low and problems develop that seem insurmountable. In fact, many people don't even believe life is worth living because they see no value in themselves and cannot see themselves as Christ sees them.

Dear Danuta:

I have heard that we must love ourselves. I do not. I have never loved myself. I cannot see one thing good about me. I have been shy all my life. I cannot talk to others. I never know what to say. I want to hide rather than talk to people. I can't even go to church. I feel like I'm ugly and people are talking about me.

My husband says he loves me, but I don't believe it. How can he love me when I can't even love myself?

Dear Feeling Unlovable:

I am sorry you do not see yourself the way God sees you. When you call yourself stupid, ugly, shy, scared, afraid, and unlovable, you are confessing the lies of Satan. In the eyes of God through your belief in Jesus Christ, you are free from those lies. Good heavens, that's why Jesus died for you!

Colossians 2:20 NIV says, "Since you died with Christ to the basic principles of this world, why, as though you still belonged to it, do you submit to its rules." Colossians 1:13 says, "He has delivered us from the power of darkness and translated us into the kingdom of the Son of His love."

If you don't believe that in the eyes of God you are beautiful, then you do not believe God. You are listening to the enemy. Here is a promise from God Himself. James 4:7 says, "Therefore submit to God. Resist the devil and he will flee from you." Now, that is a promise. It doesn't matter what you believe and it doesn't matter what I believe about you. What matters is what God believes. What matters is that Jesus finds you special.

Practice saying some nice things about yourself and be on His side for a change.

Dear Danuta:

People tell me I am attractive, pleasant, and intelligent. But when I look in the mirror, I'm always seeing something wrong. I can't seem to forgive myself for just being me. I keep thinking if I could just change something about my physical appearance, or if I wasn't so quiet, or if I could talk different, maybe people would like me. I just don't feel comfortable talking to people.

I feel other people's reactions to me are more important than my own opinions of myself. I used to feel like a winner. Now I feel like a loser or a freak.

All I really want is to be able to help others and *just be myself* without feeling bad about it.

Dear Worried About Others:

After reading your letter, it was quite clear that you *are* more concerned about what other people think of you than what you think of yourself. In fact, it almost seems that you are making a bigger deal out of your shyness than they are.

You know Jesus died for you because He loved you. Would you dare to tell Him that you're not worth loving if He gave His whole life for you?

You sound like the attractive, intelligent and pleasant person others see in you. Why not prove that you can be self-confident as well? Do not despair, for despair only leads to inaction. In despair there is no hope and no reason to act. But there *is* hope in what Christ can do with your life. You can do anything with Him.

Perhaps it's time to become independent and gain a foothold as a productive individual. *Actions always speak louder than words.* What you *do* is more important than what you think or what anyone else thinks. Get active, get involved in life. Join a swim club. Visit a hospital or a senior citizens' home. Become a "Big Sister" to a needy child.

Climb up out of the dumps. Take one step at a time. Write a plan of action for your life on a piece of paper. Then get on with life and enjoy it.

Dear Danuta:

Last fall I wrote to you because my life was literally falling apart. At that time I told you of my broken engagement to a man I loved so much and how I thought that God "played favorites" among His people.

I also told you how unfair it was for me to be thirty-two years old, never married, and feeling very lonely. I even hated my job, which I had had for eight years. I never knew anyone could hold so much bitterness for God and life itself.

Then, a few weeks later, I got a long letter from you. It told me how you would pray for me and my life. Well, to be honest with you, Danuta, I thought you would forget about my depressing letter and get on with your life. Boy, was I wrong! I never dreamed that there is so much power in reaching out to someone who really does care.

And now I want to update you on my life. In July I was married! My husband and I live in a new city, and we couldn't be any happier. Everything just fell into place when I asked for your prayers, and I began to pray myself.

Thank you so much, Danuta. You'll never know how much I appreciate your concern for me at a time when I needed it so much.

Dear Grateful:

What a blessing and a joy it was to read your precious letter! I appreciate your taking the time to let me know that the Lord has indeed worked things out in your life. Stay near to Him; continue to pray; keep Him as the Lord of your life. Never let the cares and temptations of life tear you away from a closeness to Him.

Blessings to you and your new husband.

Why am I so depressed?

Dear Danuta:

I have a physical illness that is worse than I let on to be. I learned that complaining was detrimental to my family, so I just suffer in silence.

But I am deeply depressed. I cannot bear the dark shadows that sneak up before I know it. I have cried myself to sleep many times in agony wondering how much longer I can endure this. The dark shadows are so difficult to deal with.

Dear Depressed:

I appreciate your sharing with me your feelings about depression and physical illness.

Depression very often is the result of self-pity. Self-pity can sneak in through physical illness that is painful and disabling. We feel disappointed in our situation; then self-pity comes in and hope goes out the door. Self-pity overcomes us and warps our thinking. We feel justified in having a pity party. Full-blown depression results. Self-pity becomes a way of life—a habit.

Habits need to be dealt with. Jesus said, in effect, "If anyone wants to follow me, he must deny himself. . . ." Deny yourself the right to pity yourself. Turn self-pity around. Thank God for your illness. Thank Him for being just the way you are; then thank Him for being with you in all your circumstances. Be glad. Rejoice. Develop an attitude of gratitude to Him. Pray for this change of attitude to come about, and He'll help you. You need to share your feelings with your family. Don't hold everything inside. There's a difference between complaining and explaining. Let your family share your pain. Help them understand what you're going through.

I'm looking forward to hearing how God answers your prayers.

I want to change—but how?

*Some people realize a change is needed, and can even iden-
tify what they would rather be doing . . . but they still don't
seem to be able to bridge the gap from inertia to positive action. Many times it is a matter of priorities—shifting from
what is thought to be important to what really is important
can seem to be a monumental task. "Trust in God" is a
simple phrase but a powerful medicine!*

Dear Danuta:

I am single, female, and twenty-eight years old. I still live at
home. I am a college graduate, but my job is dull and my salary is
not great. I am a spirit-filled Christian. I pray. I read my Bible. I
give to the church.

Despite being a Christian, I feel unfulfilled. I feel my life is
going nowhere. I have few friends and no social life because of
my crazy working hours. I have frequent periods of depression
and a low self-image. Nothing seems to be exciting or enjoyable
to me anymore. Why do I feel like such a flop?

Dear Unfulfilled:

The answer to your letter is rather simple. You say that your
job is dull, your salary low. Suggestion: Get an exciting job with a
good salary. You say that you have few friends. Suggestion: Start
reaching out to people and making some friends. See their needs
and try to fill them. You say that your social life is the pits. Get
new hours. Frequent periods of depression? A low self-image?
Who wouldn't with the kind of situation you have put yourself
into!

Nothing seems exciting or enjoyable in your life because nothing *is* exciting or enjoyable. It's time for action. If you really want your life to change from boring to wonderful, it's as simple as making it happen.

You have a college degree—what's keeping you from getting a new job with better hours and pay? Nothing in town you want to do? Move to another town. If you want friends, you'll have to make them. You have to listen to them, help them, reach out to them. You have to be the kind of friend you yourself want to have.

You sound like a little bird trapped in a cage. You're a big girl now. Get out of your cage. Spread your wings and try to fly. Take risks with your imagination. Dare to think. Dare to dream. Dare to give your complacency a swift kick. The biggest battle you have is with yourself and with your willingness to let things stay the way they are.

Write me with news of your plans.

Dear Danuta:

I put all my time and effort into my job and neglected my family for years. I became very successful and finally became one of the youngest executives of my company. My problem developed when I just didn't know how to love my wife. I constantly lusted after other women and soon I was demoted from my job. Yet no matter how I tried, the lust wouldn't go away. I went into counseling, but I fell again and made sexual remarks to a woman at work. A letter was written, and because I was warned before, I was terminated from my job.

I keeping asking God to forgive me again and again. We had only just moved into our new home three weeks before when I was called into headquarters and terminated. It has been eight weeks now and after two job interviews, I still don't have a job. I've asked for forgiveness and have prayed for a healing. I never want to be like my old self.

I'm really struggling now. Not just financially, but spiritually and emotionally. I know I must renew everything. But I'm afraid to lose my home and possessions. I'm afraid to lose my family. I want so much to be the father and husband God wants me to be. Can you help me?

Dear Afraid to Lose:

I have received your desperate letter, and feel so very sorry about your position; but I want to tell you that this could be a tremendous time for you.

During our most despairing times we are promised that *all* things come together for good to those who love God. In that simple promise, you can believe that if you lose it all . . . house, home, job, income, IF you trust completely in God, He will see you through and turn events around. Sometimes, we have to "clean house," get rid of all our bad habits, in order to rearrange the furniture of our lives! Perhaps you are being nudged into a new place, a new level of understanding, literally and spiritually.

In relying on God, you must resolve entirely to be willing to give up everything. You must TRUST in His will for you and not your own. That's a tough assignment. But if you can let go of your possessions and your home for His sake . . . HE WILL MOVE.

He may move you from where you live. He may move your spirit to a whole new dimension. The Lord may be readjusting your priorities from yourself and your career to your wife and family. Sometimes there is pain involved with uprooting the old man and transplanting the new man. But Christ will not fail you for doing what is right and good and true.

This could be a time for you and your wife to draw closer to each other and to the Lord. Do you and your wife pray together?

Read the Word together? Do you go to church together? All of these would give you another step in changing the direction of your life.

Be assured as well that if you have asked for forgiveness, you have received it. Be assured of His unending love for you.

The way out of a cobweb is to unravel it one strand at a time. Begin with rededicating your life to Christ. All other things will follow. I am convinced you are about to embark on a great spiritual adventure. Hold on; He won't let you fall.

———

Dear Danuta:

I need to change my life.

I have a desire and a need to teach full time. I have taught school for fifteen years and stayed at home for ten. But I cannot find a job.

I am tired of being under a mountain of debt. I've been trying to lose weight because I am tired of being in bondage to fat. I want to find a place to teach.

Can you give me some advice about getting control of my diet, my finances, and my career?

Dear Needing Change:

I have good news for you.

Wanting change is the first step in having change. You know you want a teaching job. You know that you want to lose weight, and you know that you want to get out of debt. Take each goal one step at a time. Write out your plan of action on a piece of paper and then follow it. Sounds too simple to believe, huh? But the hardest part of reaching your goal is sticking to it. Your letter is full of wishes, but I can see no practical methods for making your wishes come true.

To get a teaching job, you need to compile and send out resumés. You need to make your presence known to people in authority and to keep at it.

To lose weight, start exercising—stay away from fats, sweets, and caffeine. Join a spa and get on a weight-loss program with the health-care professionals there.

To get out of debt, write out a budget and stick to it. Try consolidating your debts. Pay your debtors off little by little. Call your creditors and tell them your plan. They'd love to get their money, so they'll listen to what you say.

Perseverance is the key. Prayer is the answer. Make yourself out a plan and go for it.

———————

Dear Danuta:

I am writing to say THANKS! Of course, I realize you don't know me and probably don't even know what you did. But you did a lot.

Let me tell you.

When I was unemployed most of the summer, the "700 Club" was the one bright spot in my day. Somehow it really lifted me. It was you especially who seemed to have such a cheering effect on me. Just to tune in and see your smile and your happy personality perked me up. Of course I know it is the Lord who really ministers through all of you at the "700 Club." But I was really touched and blessed by you in a special way.

Even more than "thank you," all I can say is that "God used you!" I know that will mean a lot to you.

Your sister in Christ

P.S. After much prayer I got a job in a wonderful new store and am learning fashion design—a whole new field for me!

Dear Sister:

Your precious letter gave a real lift to my spirit. I am so glad that you like the program and that God has been able to use it to bless you.

Blessings to you in your new position.

———————

What's so wrong about homosexuality?

One day while a group of friends and I were having a re-union over dinner, one of the women at the table announced she was going to get married. Everyone rejoiced with her until she announced that she was going to marry another woman! A loud gasp filled the air from her unsaved friends, but the shock led to support and before long everyone at the table had surrounded their friend and was offering the services of a florist, a printer for the invitations, and a photographer for the event.

I was the only one who sat still at the table. Later, I wrote her the following letter.

My Dear and Precious Friend:

Among all your friends, most of whom support you, I must be the one "lone voice in the wilderness" amongst them saying that what you are doing is wrong—not in my judgment, but in God's eyes. If no one else will speak the truth, I must.

Your pals say that they want "whatever makes you happy." They might not want to confront the morality of your decision because they didn't want to offend or embarrass you. Another explanation for their support is the belief that truth, morality, or ethics are situational and subjective rather than absolute.

My prayer is that I can respond to these rationalizations in a logical manner that will show you that the support of many is vastly outweighed by the voice of God.

"Whatever makes you happy" is not the most important objective in life; on the contrary, what makes you happy is *not* necessarily what is best for you. A heroin addict with a needle jammed in his arm and feeling the warm ooze from his fix is happy! But is that really what's good for him? In the long run, that sort of "happiness" is fleeting. It is a momentary sensation, an elevated or exaggerated perspective activated by an emotional or physical need and satisfied by a corresponding emotional or physical response.

Now, please understand that I am not against your being happy. However, I am against the phrase "whatever makes you happy." "Whatever" means *anything* you do. A child may be happy playing in the street, but obviously his happiness is outweighed by the danger from the cars in the street. Your happiness today may very well jeopardize not only your life tomorrow, but your relationship with God.

I submit to you that joy is more lasting than happiness: it is an inner peace that comes from knowing you are beloved of God, that you don't *need* anybody or anything to maintain that joy. Joy is not as superfluous and is far more sustaining than happiness because joy does not rely on something or someone else for its existence. People and things are temporal, and so are their effects on us. God is permanent, and so is His joy.

But now for the nitty-gritty . . . the morality of your choice. No one likes to speak of morality these days: people like to say, "If it feels good, it's right." Somehow the word *moral* has become a bad word, the distasteful consideration, the embarrassing code of behavior, the old-fashioned objection, the affliction of a minority, the unscientific, nonprogressive, antiquated opinion. That I stand on the anachronism of God's love may make my odd position somewhat curious to you and, therefore, worth hearing if only for its audacity.

Let me explain by first pointing out a remarkable phenomenon. Did you notice that at the very moment you said you were involved in a gay relationship, for a split second there was silence among your friends? The gasp was surprise . . . the silence was the tiny voice of truth, the small voice of God—the moral acknowledgement that something was wrong. But then suddenly, wanting to appear cool and popular, everyone crushed that tiny conviction in a wave of modern sentiment and misguided love for you. But friendship is more than a popularity contest or playing the role of the flatterer. As your friend, I cannot encourage you, but must warn you. You are walking down a path vehemently censored by God Himself!

> "Do you know that the unrighteous will not inherit the kingdom of God? Do not be deceived. Neither fornicators, nor idolators, nor adulterers, nor homosexuals, nor sodomites . . . will inherit the kingdom of God." (1 Corinthians 6:9, 10)

That's pretty strong stuff! The Word of God continues . . .

> "Every sin that a man does is outside the body, but he who commits sexual immorality sins against his own body . . . the temple of the Holy Spirit . . . bought at a price . . ." (1 Corinthians 6:18-20)

Or how about this one:

> ". . . immoral men and homosexuals . . . [are] contrary to sound teaching, according to the glorious gospel of the blessed God, with which I have been entrusted." (1 Timothy 1:10, 11 NAS)

The Bible, Old and New Testaments, is *filled* with this warning. Any "minister" who tries to tap dance out of it is a liar. You would have to be blind not to see it. There are just too many references against the behavior to ignore. If one *chooses* to ignore God's warning, then one is treating His Word like a smorgasbord . . . "I'll take a little of this and a little of that . . . but I'll leave out the parts I don't like."

It all boils down to this . . . either you walk with God or you don't. You either accept Him or you don't. There is no shade of gray! There *are* such distinctions as right and wrong, and as long as you accept *that,* you must buy it *all the way.* Not as far as you *like* it, or as far as it makes you happy. You must not be lukewarm about this. Revelation 3:16 says, "So then, because you are lukewarm, and neither cold nor hot, I will spew you out of My mouth."

It's pretty clear. Truth is not what you want it to be. Truth is not a subjective noun. Truth depends neither on one's perspective nor one's situation. Yet, it is so easy to fall into the trap of "cognitive dissonance" . . . that is, making attempts at justifying one's position by either changing the facts or changing your perspective of the facts in order to suit your position.

The good news is this. If you will follow God, He will give you everything: joy unspeakable, peace that passes all understanding, the very desires of your heart. Rewards and satisfactions—joy that lasts. All these things I have written to you are promises. Guarantees. God Himself has promised great things for us IN THIS WORLD as well as the next, but we must first make the commitment to Him. You can't get a better deal than a promise from the Creator of the universe!

The bad news is this: If you, with full conscience and understanding of His love, willfully choose to live outside His commandments, and walk down a path filled with justifications and compromises with conveniently twisted truths where the immoral becomes the moral, where self-made rights usurp righteousness— to whom will you turn when your castle of sand crumbles around you? Who will answer in the darkness of the place in which you choose to dwell?

You are too precious to lose to this deception of "happiness" and you're too smart to be so easily fooled.

Dear friend, it's up to you to choose now, fully equipped with knowledge of right and wrong and the consequences each choice holds . . . I beg you—choose joy!

How can I kick
this awful habit?

Dear Danuta:

I need you to pray for me. My husband has left me. I need help to raise my two boys, as my parents are aged.

I especially need help to stop my cigarette habit, as it is a waste of money. It makes my mother ill. She is sixty-four and is allergic to smoke. My father has had two throat operations and my smoking isn't good for him, either. I know it sets a bad example for my two sons. I want so much to stop smoking.

Dear Needing Help to Stop:

My heart is deeply touched by the distress you are experiencing. Yes, I pray now for you, for your husband, for your two sons, and for your parents who share in your distress.

Be strong in the Lord and in the power of His might. As you read this letter, throw all the cigarettes you have on the floor and smash them with your feet—then throw them away. At the same time you throw them down, declare this: "In the name of Jesus Christ I bind the spirit of nicotine in my life. I now receive deliverance from the smoking habit. I give it up. I am free in Jesus' name."

Instead of smoking, praise and thank the Lord daily, over and over, for setting you free. It is most important that you sincerely desire to quit smoking. With Christ's help, you now can. If you have the habit of smoking in a certain chair—avoid the chair. If you smoke after a meal, go for a walk instead. Chew gum. Take a bath. Wash the dog. Busy yourself each time you feel like smoking. Try running. There's nothing more difficult to do than trying to swallow down smoke after a run!

Ask the Lord for what you need—for what your sons need—the main need being that each of your boys commit his life to Christ. Pray with them. He will help you because He loves you.

Dear Danuta:

I have been addicted to Valium for five years. I decided to quit after watching your program.

Have I been tempted to take Valium again? Definitely yes! However, each time the temptation comes upon me, I ask God to help me overcome the desire.

I thank God for His concern and for your gift.

Dear Overcoming Temptation:

You are special and don't ever forget that fact! You are so special that the Lord knows even the numbers of the hairs of your head. He cares for you deeply, more than He does for the birds of the air whom He feeds, not one of which falls to the ground without His knowledge. Do you get the Message?

He wants your life, not just so He can overcome for you the addiction to Valium, but so that He can mold you into the woman He created you to be. But your task is to take hands off your life and yield yourself without reservation to Him like clay to the potter. His desire is to transform each of us into a vessel which is useful to mankind and, therefore, to the cause of Christ. Be that clay.

Dear Danuta:

I am addicted to Darvon and have been for almost fifteen years. I know that I am not living the kind of life God wants me to, but I am not sure I am willing to give up the desire I have for this painkiller. I don't know why I cannot give this problem over to Jesus.

I am thirty-five years old, have been married twice, and am so empty inside it is unbelievable. Why is it that I cannot escape this drug and this terrible depression?

Dear Empty:

You have to make a choice. You either choose God or you choose Darvon. You either believe in the power of the Creator of the universe or you believe in the power of the pill. You are either ready for your life to be meaningful or you're content with emptiness. It's very easy to be dissatisfied with your life. But it takes work to do something about it.

And sometimes it's easier to be complacent than it is to make changes.

To get your act together, go to a drug rehabilitation center, your doctor, or a local hospital. Then, after you get help, don't quit until you're clean. Your life can radically change if you choose it. Your emptiness can be filled with love. But *you* have to initiate change.

Do one completely selfless thing for someone else and see how you feel. Then do it again. You get love by giving it away. There are so many people in need. Get some Christian friends who will support you when you need it. Learn how to pray with them.

Rebuild. Begin now. Today. This minute.

I stole some money—
what should I do?

Dear Danuta:

I am writing because I am at the end of my rope. I am scared to death. My husband doesn't know what I've done. I would never want him to find out. I have two wonderful children who could be hurt by this too.

It all started when I needed money to pay bills. I had to get it, so I took some money from my company. Then when payday came, I needed more. When Christmas came, I had no money for the children, and the landlord wanted all the past rent money right away. So I stole more money from work.

I counted all the money I have taken and it comes to $2,000. Can you imagine a Christian doing such a thing? You don't know how guilty and sorry I am.

Now I am so scared my boss will find out. I'm scared every time the phone rings. It has gotten to the point where I can think of nothing else. I can't believe I failed God and my family in this way. What should I do?

Dear Scared to Death:

Your problem is obviously unbearable. The guilt and regret which you suffer have already outweighed the temporary relief that dishonesty affords. Dishonesty never allows a God-fearing person the fruits of inner peace because the spirit is disregarding its own convictions. Guilt and regret are cancerous. They will only get worse and breed difficulties and problems you haven't even imagined yet! I believe that you are an honest person asking for forgiveness. If you weren't, your letter would never have been written.

God forgives; unfortunately the law does not. This is your dilemma. Sometimes it seems that people are less understanding than God, making confession a painful, punitive process. But it doesn't have to be that way. God wants your honesty back, and the company will want its money back and it will find out how to get it one way or another. But God has already forgiven you, so you're halfway there.

Now for the legal and personal aspects of your problem. First, you *have* to talk to your husband. You need his support in this. You should not face this alone because the consequences could affect him as well. Second, you have to pray together. Pray for a resolution to this problem. Pray for guidance and for wisdom. But do it together. Third, with your husband by your side, talk to your employer and tell him what you have done. Now this can be hard but it doesn't have to be impossible. Realize that this could cost you your job. But isn't losing your job far better than what you're going through now? Finally, talk to a lawyer. Having arranged a repayment schedule with your employer, a lawyer will help to protect you legally.

These are tough answers, but it was a tough question. God bless you. Be strong, have faith in God, and He'll take care of you.

———————

Do I have to look like this?

Dear Danuta:

I'm the wife of a very successful businessman. His job has given me wonderful opportunities to witness to people. Yet I know these people cannot have any respect for what I might say to them when they see I have not been able to do anything about my weight problem. It's gotten so that I now stay home from all social activities. I can't move from my chair.

My weight problem has ruined the last thirty years of my life. All my precious young years are behind me. If I'm not healed soon, it won't matter anymore. I'd be better off dead than to have to face another twenty years of dieting. I'm convinced I'm never going to be helped.

Dear Convinced:

It's a brand-new year ahead and I want you to know that the Lord Jesus Christ loves you enough to have died for you. If you were the only person in the world, that dear Savior would still have perished on a wooden cross in agony for you alone.

While I read your letter, I couldn't shake the feeling that you are under attack by Satan because of the opportunities you have to spread the name of Jesus. You are obviously a powerful witness for Him, and I have noticed that the more powerful a person is for the Lord, the more serious the attack from the adversary. Your weight is keeping you from the Lord, and this is exactly what Satan has in mind. Obviously, it's working.

The very fact that you won't even go outside is an indication that you are feeding the problem rather than solving the problem.

The more inactive and ashamed you become, the more serious your problem becomes. You have to start living as though you have victory. You have to start praying the promises of God rather than praying about your problem. You are not told to sit on a chair and watch all your brothers and sisters in Christ having a good time; that's not the way it goes. The way it goes is this: Jesus wants all of us to get out there and enjoy life and enjoy His Kingdom. You are restricting yourself to the chair; you, with the help of Satan. Don't give in to him! Praise God! Use a lot of praise in your prayers and start living as though the victory and the promise of health are yours. LIVE AS THOUGH THEY ARE YOURS. You will find that Satan will be defeated. Claim the Blood of Jesus. Claim His name every time you pray to God.

We often have to get outside ourselves to solve our problems. It seems as though you are far too involved in your problem to really see how to get it solved. Step out of yourself, start ministering to others, and don't let Satan have his hand over you in this case. When he leaves, your life will be new again. Just have faith in God!

If during this next year you feel grief, guilt, terrible hurt, sadness, despair, or unrelenting self-criticism, you should know that that is not from God. That is from the adversary. Satan will use every trick in the book including all your weaknesses, all your fears, and all your condemnations about dieting. Stop dieting; it doesn't work. Start living—fully. Exercise, *move,* get active. Think *less* of yourself (and your weight) and think more of others. *Avoid* foods that will harm your health, but don't get paranoid about it—that only leads to obsessive *self*ness. . . . And you need to get off your problems and involved in other people instead. It works!

I'm convinced that the Lord is going to heal you this year. You must know that too. You must hear it, and you must believe it. Do away with all this self-condemnation. Sweep it out of your life. This is a year of victory for you.

You are a child of God and He loves you very much.

Dear Danuta:

You're the one who "hooked" me on the show. You're not a saccharine, submissive, bubbleheaded bit of fluff, but a REAL WOMAN. You're so sure of your femininity that you feel free to do really fun things on the show, like panning for gold or using a bulldozer to level an outhouse.

This year, I've decided to set in motion some of the goals I've wanted for myself. I'm tired of the old me. I'd love to have your poise, grace, and taste. I'd love especially to have your special look. Can you give the "new me" some tips on improving my appearance?

Dear New Me:

Thank you so much for your kind letter. I feel rather honored that you would use me as an example of "poise, grace, and taste." Who, me? The klutz?

In any case, I think I can help you with a little advice. My "look" didn't come too easily. It took patience and work and a desire to change the old to the new. Sometimes we get rather comfortable with the "old us" and in spite of the willingness to want to change . . . something always tells us that it's more secure to be the old and familiar than the new and uncommon. So changing your attitude comes first. Second, hire an image consultant. They usually don't cost a lot of money, and the investment is INVALUABLE. In fact, the one hundred fifty dollars I invested in my image consultant will remain with me for the rest of my life. She organized my closet, threw out the clothes I shouldn't get caught dead in, and made a list of the colors and items I needed to complete a suitable wardrobe on the budget I could afford! Then she began to advise me on makeup techniques and colors and hair. It took courage to trust her, but her information lingers. Now every time I go shopping alone, I can coordinate outfits with amazing versatility—and my clothing dollar goes a lot further! Never buy clothes item by item, but think of clothing that coordinates with numerous things in your closet.

Goals are extremely important, and you're on the right track there! Joyful living is also an asset. When you know when to rest, and when you can rely on the Lord for guidance . . . you don't need to worry about things . . . and the joy shines through without obstruction.

Dear Danuta:
Something has been bothering me but I'm too embarrassed to tell anyone. However, I'm going to tell you.

Two blocks from where I work is a tattoo parlor. A year ago, after I broke up with a man, I went in and had "VANITY" tattooed on my abdomen where it would not be on display to the general public. I didn't do it to be tattooed, but I thought I needed to be reminded daily to hold my head high with self-esteem. But then I became a Christian and now I look at my stomach every day with despair. The letters are so big!

I've heard that having a tattoo removed is very painful. I've thought about having an *X* tattooed through it but VANITY would still show through. I've thought of having "is sin" added. But think of all that writing on my stomach!

The only idea I've come up with is "ask Danuta." Danuta, what would you do if you had mistakenly tattooed VANITY on your stomach? Would you have it removed? Or wear a Band-Aid the rest of your life? Vanity does not show through any sincere Christian. Conversion can change your deeds and your heart, but what do you do about your tattoo?

Well, Danuta, I guess strange letters sometimes come through the mail, and I suppose this is one. But I'm sincere. Please answer.

Dear Sincere:

I thought I had heard everything, but this takes the cake!

Removing your tattoo through plastic surgery may be a possibility. Dermabrasion is another. I am not certain about the guarantee that the tattoo would be completely lifted by the latter. Contact a plastic surgeon; that is my first advice.

Otherwise, I would advise you to live with it, and every time you look at it, be reminded that vanity is akin to pride, the greatest of all sins, which was the cause of the fall of a beautiful angel.

Pride has caused the greatest inhumanities and atrocities ever conceived. Pride has toppled nations, set man against man, bred war and disease. Pride provoked the Holocaust, the arms race, the atomic bomb. We have killed, murdered, robbed, and raped because of pride. To pride we owe the avarice of materialism and the lust for a neighbor's spouse. Envy, debt, poverty, and greed are the sons of pride. It is the sin of sins; it blinds and separates us from God. It is the attempt to replace our Creator with ourselves.

You have indelibly reminded yourself of a great knowledge, and more than most, you will be aware of your need for Christ, who washes the sin from our souls. No plastic surgeon can do that!

How can I meet Mr. Right?

So many Christian women who write to me feel obsessed with the idea of getting married. It seems as though they put their lives on hold, believing that life begins at marriage and until then they are only half-people.

The biggest mistake these women can make is believing that if they are bored now, they will be fulfilled when they get married. Or that if they are lonely and friendless now, marriage will solve the dilemma. Or if they are depressed or without a goal or sense of meaning in life, Mr. Right will make it right!

Marriage complicates; it doesn't simplify. Many times it can create more problems for people who have not discovered their own God-given uniqueness. How many times have we heard the wife's lament, "I need to find out who I am!" as she rushes out of a marriage to "discover" herself?

For a marriage to be successful, you need two successful people. By "successful," I mean personally at ease with themselves, with their lives, with their love and understanding of Jesus, and with each other. Spiritual, physical, mental, and emotional grounding, when then incorporated into another person's life, adds rather than subtracts from the relationship. In this way, the marriage entertains two happy, purposeful people, each of whom loves God, enjoys His world, and brings this sense of wonder to the other.

Dear Danuta:

I'm single, will be twenty-nine this year, and want to marry a Christian man. When you married Kai, I was thrilled for you.

You see, I realize that you're not in your twenties and you married a beautiful man—that gave me hope.

Sometimes, Danuta, I just want to be held by someone who loves me. I dream of having babies and I yearn for companionship, for someone I can do things with.

Dear Wanting to Be Held:

Being twenty-nine years old and not yet married does not mean it will never happen. Wait on the Lord; the effort will be worth it. I'm a perfect example of that. Along with every other single person on this earth, I know how long and lonely the nights can be. At one time or another, we all get lonely and want to be held by someone.

Yet it has occurred to me that when a woman becomes totally consumed by the idea of "catching" a man, her life becomes pretty boring. All her interests, her hobbies, come to a screeching halt, waiting . . . her whole life is put on hold while waiting for the perfect man to make life worth living. The problem is that if you are not a fully satisfied woman now, no person will make you completely satisfied as a woman. You are in for a big disappointment.

Looking back just three years, I realize that I never wanted to marry. I always considered marriage a hindrance, an obstacle to the achievement of my goals—my education and my career. I believed that if I were to marry, either my career or my marriage would suffer neglect, and I was right! During the time I was putting myself through school and trying to get a head start in my career in broadcasting, any deterrent would have made me less than what I had always dreamed of becoming: a success.

But then, I met the Lord. And then my career took second place. My education was under my belt and working for CBN fulfilled the goal for meaningful work for Jesus. I was a success; I had achieved my goals for satisfaction and meaning in my life. I was content. I was ready for companionship and the Lord knew it! I reminded Him once in a while in prayer, but I didn't harp on it. I didn't cling to the misery of being alone. I KNEW that He KNEW and that having asked, I would receive. PERIOD. Then I went about my business as usual.

My husband is a man I had known for six long years. He was a man I wanted no interest in romantically, although he had become my best friend and confidant. I was in love with him from the moment I met him. But I built such great defenses against him since he traveled so much that I was dating anyone *but* him!

In prayer he was convinced that we would be married, and popped the question, confident that the Lord would give me the same word. Well, He didn't . . . at least, not right away. It took a week.

We offered Jesus the decision and prayed for His guidance in the matter and then simply waited. (Not an easy thing to do!)

I put out a fleece to the Lord one night . . . asking for a sign that only He and I would understand. I asked that the wind chimes that hang in my bedroom might ring if I was supposed to marry Kai. I waited and waited, and fell asleep in the silence of the room.

Boy, what a stupid thing to do, I thought!

Four days later, still immobilized by indecision, I woke up in the middle of the night with a warm glow running through my body, and a perceptible HOT SPOT flickering deep within my breast. I gasped out loud and said audibly, "I think I'm falling in love with Kai!" As I spoke the words . . . those wind chimes that had never rung began to chime in the darkness. They rang for several minutes before stopping! I thought I was dreaming, or at least going out of my mind! The next day, *I* proposed to *him*!

What I'm trying to tell you is this: Rejoice in your life today. Get involved with activities, hobbies, the theater, art classes, gardening, scuba diving. The more involved you are in life the more attractive you will become to people of the opposite sex. You may have to fight them off with a stick. But men know when a woman is looking for a man and they'll run.

Dear Danuta:

It's been eight years since I divorced my second husband ... eight years of loneliness without a mate. In that time, I have not felt accepted in a society based on marriage and family. I try not to complain but I miss married life.

My constant prayer is that the Lord will grant me a good Christian husband. This home needs a man's strength. I need help with many chores because I am fifty-five. I have been so hurt by my husbands. I long to remarry someone who will best complement me in the Lord, but I am afraid.

Dear Without a Mate:

It is time to let go of the past. Let go of the pain. Let go of the hurt. It's time for a new life in Christ. Embrace life. Enjoy life. Join clubs and groups which are doing things you love to do. Find some friends and go fishing, horseback riding, camping; enroll in some adult education classes, get involved in Bible study and church activities. Take up jogging; join a spa. Get involved with life. As you embrace life, all of life will embrace you. You will become attractive to many people who will just love to be with you because you will exude life and love and all that Jesus has to offer. That's the best advice that I can give to anyone.

Dear Danuta:

I am almost twenty-seven and have never dated. Guess I'm hoping for the perfect man or none at all. Your network's been showing features on my favorite Christian, Cliff Richard. I've been a fan of his for ten years or so, at least since the hit single "Devil Woman."

I've been praying for a husband in a way—but not just any

husband. I've been praying for Cliff! Laugh if you want to. Only God and my mother known how much I love him.

I am very bored and lonely. I've been to college and I can't get a job doing anything. So I've stopped looking for one.

My dad has never encouraged me. My mom's been very good to me. But I have high ideals and I can't tell her how I feel. I don't like the TV much anymore, or even the radio. Now I hardly ever play my music.

I'm going nowhere fast. I'm missing out on everything. What can I do, Danuta? I need someone to inspire me, to care for me, and to understand me. Perhaps I'm not supposed to get married. But if I did, I'd want him to be Cliff Richard or someone exactly like him.

Dear Missing Out:

When I was a little girl, I was madly in love with Dr. Kildare on TV and my little heart went flippity-flop every time I saw the actor who played him, Richard Chamberlain. Of all the men I wanted to marry, he was Mr. Right. Fortunately, I grew up and was able to tell the difference between fantasy and reality. It's time you did the same.

You sound as though your everyday life is so disappointing ("I'm going nowhere fast. I'm missing out on everything") that you're beginning to prefer fantasy to reality.

Your chances of meeting Cliff Richard are astronomically slim, and if that's what you're hanging your life on, your chances for happiness are also slim.

The Bible is the living Word of God and Jesus is the only One you can lean on 100 percent. It's time to get your life in order and your priorities straight. Find goals that you wish to attain and write them down. Create plans to achieve those goals and then carry them through. With Jesus as your "guiding star" you can have a happy life.

Get on with it.

I'm old—
do I have to be lonely, too?

Loneliness is a common complaint in our society. And many people write about the pain that loneliness brings to their lives. It takes work to battle that insipid disease, which can actually sap the will to live from its victims.

Jesus is the living God. He cares about us and He is with us always. With His grace and inspiration, loneliness can be turned into a motivation for productive and positive action.

Dear Danuta:

I am a widow, seventy-six years old, and have a forty-seven-year-old unmarried daughter. We are both lonely and set in our ways. The problem is that my daughter's rent has been raised, and she would like me to come and live with her. I want to help her out but I'm so worried that it won't work out. Every time I stay with her a week, it so upsets her that she makes me cry.

Danuta, my friend, what should I do?

Dear Wanting to Help:

Two lonely women together equals two lonely women. You both need your own lives and ending loneliness does not come about by doubling it. It doesn't necessarily come from physical circumstances either, but from a decision made inside you.

If you are lonely, do some volunteer work. Visit other lonely people in hospitals and nursing homes. Bake them some goodies to cheer them up. Maybe a child care center nearby could use some help. Perhaps there's some work at your church that you could dive into. My point is this—help yourself by helping others.

Get yourself a little dog. But don't move in with your daughter. Misery may like company, but you don't need it. You could chew each other up within a year.

Your daughter needs her life too. She needs to start reaching out and getting involved with life. If she is having difficulty now, it would be double jeopardy to live with Mother.

Go with your intuition; you may be right. If you suspect that moving in with your daughter could be a problem, it probably will be. You just wanted me to tell you what you already know.

Dear Danuta:

My beloved wife left me to live with the Lord two years ago. We had fifty-seven years of wedded bliss together. I sure miss the dear girl.

I am eighty-two and it is a lonesome life as I sit here all day with nobody to talk to but my dog.

Dear Wedded Bliss:

How wonderful that you enjoyed fifty-seven years of marriage to somebody you loved so much! I know that you must miss her terribly. As you reflect about your time together, I wonder if it wouldn't be a good idea to get yourself a little dictaphone and to speak into it the highlights of your life with her. Perhaps you should write a story about your marriage that might inspire young people as they struggle with their marriages. You could probably get a high school student or perhaps a counselor from the "700 Club" to write down your words. Also, maybe you could find an editor and eventually a publisher and put your life into book form. You sound as if you have a lot of insight that would be so beneficial to others.

What can I do about the pain?

Dear Danuta:

I had to go to the emergency room last week because the pain in my back was so bad. My spine is loaded with arthritis. The doctors gave me a lot of shots and medications. But nothing helps. I guess it's just not time for me to be healed. Even though the pain is unbearable at times, I still praise His name.

Please pray that I will have the strength to stand the pain.

Dear Waiting for Healing:

When I experience a lot of pain, I always remind myself of the pain Jesus endured for me. He was whipped; the hair was pulled from his face and head; he was beaten to a bloody pulp, *nailed* to a cross, and hoisted naked to die in agony. My pain is so much less than His! And when He died He took my pain upon His own body. With those thoughts I offer my pain to Him. Somehow, pain lessens; and peace is all around me.

I think you're on the right track when you say that you'll praise the Lord regardless of the circumstances, but we are also the victims of our wills and can choose to be tormented. In fact, torment is one of the things that we do best to ourselves. Make room for more love and more praise and throw the torment out the window. Along with Job in chapter 13, verse 15, make this your statement of faith: "Though He slay me, yet will I trust Him."

Jesus will heal you. Until He does, offer your pain as a sacrifice—and use it as a vehicle to touch the pain of Christ. In a mysterious paradox, you will come to know His love for you through the pain you *both* endure.

And there is another aspect to pain that comes from within ourselves. Sometimes emotional pain from past or present circumstances breeds inside us and manifests itself in physical torment. If there is something in your life that has crippled you, you must release it—emotionally and spiritually. Release comes through forgiveness. If you forgive, regardless of whose "fault" it was or is, and offer your forgiveness *in earnest* to Christ—He will take the pain and replace it with His sweet peace. Don't cling to the memories of the past. Live in the promises of the present and the hope for the future.

Wouldn't I be better off dead?

Someone once said that suicide is a permanent solution to a temporary problem. There are those who write who are in the depths of great despair, and that desperation clouds all sense of proportion. If they could step back for just a brief time from those overwhelming problems, their problems would be seen as mere obstacles that can be circumvented with Christ's help.

Dear Danuta:

I was divorced for six years with two children to raise. Then I married a man who was also divorced. All kinds of things went wrong. Drinking. Sex. Drugs. Money problems got out of hand. My husband developed heart problems and lost his job. On top of that, our car was wrecked.

We had to move and sell everything. But I have to face the bank because my name is on all our notes. My husband doesn't know about some of our other bills. I have had to see an attorney about the bank. I just don't know what's going to happen.

If it were not for the "700 Club," I would have killed myself. But I heard someone on the show talking to a man who wanted to kill himself and I decided to listen. I know that suicide is wrong. But I am so frightened. Pray that the Lord sends me an answer.

Dear Frightened:

You sound as if you are panicking and when people panic, they don't think too clearly.

Ask yourself what makes a Christian different from a non-

Christian in the way he handles problems. A non-Christian spins wheels, panics, and tries to control the situation, only to end up despairing, suicidal, and completely out of control. A Christian loses control on purpose. By giving over control to God, a Christian thus short circuits a crisis.

Which are you? How much are you trusting in Him? Have you utterly abandoned yourself and your problems to Christ? Do you feel a tiny spark within you that is perfectly calm? Can you see the difference between your spiritual center and the peace Christ offers in it, and your mere physical responses to a crisis? If you can see the difference, you should know that Christ is within you; you should know that you have given yourself over to Him. If you don't feel that center of calm, you are trying to control the situation too much.

But first, you and your husband have to get straight with God. This is most important before you can get straight with each other. Become a spiritual unit. Pray together, persevere, handle one problem at a time. If need be, you could claim bankruptcy and start all over again with a clean slate. Recognize what is really important. Money, possessions, bills, all the problems of this world shall pass away. Believe it or not, these are all temporary. That the two of you together have your eyes on Christ— that's what's important. He won't let the two of you down.

Dear Danuta:

I have so many problems and needs and nowhere to go for help.

I am thirty-five years old and overweight. I've never had a job, not even a prospect for one. My family treats me like a child. I have no privacy and only one pair of jeans and a blouse to wear. For the past two years I have not been out of the house. I have no desire to even get out of bed. I go from one nightgown to another nightgown. I have let myself go until I can't stand myself.

I have prayed with you, Pat Robertson, and Ben Kinchlow many times, but nothing has ever happened to me.

I just don't have any reason to want to live. But I'm afraid to die. I don't want to be where I am but I have nowhere and no one to go to. My life is absolutely nothing.

I am writing to you because this is my last chance to try and get help for myself.

Dear Last Chance:

This is an important first step—to know that your life must change and to seek help to make change happen.

When God created man, He gave us free will, the freedom to choose to live or to die and everything else in between. He gave us free will because He loves us. This means that you are responsible for your own life. Accepting Christ into your life is the major decision of your life. This you seem to have already done.

The second major step is to act on your decision. Not acting on it means that you never made the decision in the first place. It is just lip service.

Since God loves you so much, what an insult to Him that you don't love the same things He does. Jesus respects the body, the mind, and the soul so greatly that He died for them.

Now what you should do is this:

1. *Get out of your nightgown and get dressed.*
2. *Go outside.*
3. *Take a walk. Walk a half hour each day and increase the time a little bit every week.*
4. *Notice every tiny thing that God has created. Thank Him and breathe deeply.*
5. *Get one new outfit.*
6. *Find a church and attend services regularly.*
7. *Make friends there.*

8. *Find someone who needs your help. Get your mind off yourself and become involved in another's needs.*
9. *Ask your pastor to point you in the right direction for obtaining a part-time job.*
10. *Read the Bible. It is filled with God's wisdom and knowledge.*
11. *Grow from there.*

This is the most practical advice I can give you. It is time for you to become a woman. Treasure awaits you.

Part 2

*"The abundant life—
where is it?"*

Why can't my parents and I get along?

Many people write to me about difficulties in their relation-ships with parents, husbands, and wives. In part, some of their problems begin with expecting too much from these re-lationships. In fact, many times, people tend to count more on their relationships with people than their relationship with Christ.

Dear Danuta:

I'm twelve years old and I have a problem.

I have an aunt who is sixteen years old, and she's got a little baby girl. Since she has a baby and she's not married, my parents think I am going to be just like her. I look like her, and they think I act just like her. They don't trust me, even though I haven't done anything wrong.

They fuss all the time and they're driving me crazy! Please help me.

Dear Driven Crazy:

Sometimes parents want to protect us too much because they love us so much. Your parents want only the best for you and perhaps they are overreacting to your aunt's problems.

When we are young, I am sure it often seems as though the whole world is crashing in on us. Sometimes the world seems so unfair. But, hang in there. These things shall pass away.

You know Jesus said, "Just as you want men to do to you, you also do to them" (Luke 6:31). If you treat your parents with pa-tience, tolerance, and understanding and realize they love you very much, you will find they will start treating you with patience, tolerance, and understanding. In the meantime, do a lot of praying, read the Bible, and know that God knows the truth of your heart.

You sound like a sweet, sensible young lady and I'm glad you wrote.

Dear Danuta:

I am a fifteen-year-old girl with a big problem. Ever since I was eleven years old, I have dreamed of having a different mother who would hold me whenever I needed it. I just love to be held, as if I were a baby. But the only one I don't want to hold me is my own mother. I don't hate her or anything like that. I just don't want her to even touch me, and I don't know why.

Last year, I went to my friend's mother for help. She was so understanding and she did hold me. I thought it was a dream come true. But one time just didn't do it for me. Ever since that day, I have prayed for someone to hold me.

Is there something wrong with me? Why do I feel this way about my mother? And why haven't the pain and longing gone away?

Dear Pain and Longing:

I am so glad you wrote to me because admitting that there is a problem is your first real step to getting it solved.

Something is going on inside of you that hurts too much to remember or to talk about. You need to talk to someone who is trained in uncovering hurt. That someone could be a school counselor or a favorite teacher. A psychologist would be best because he or she knows how to help you work out your feelings.

If you continue feeling this way without getting help, you will end up wanting hugs from people who don't have your best interests at heart. There could be a lot of hurt down the road for you.

Nip this problem in the bud and talk to someone who can help. God answers prayer through other people. He may be answering your prayer through my letter. Talk to someone, dear one.

Dear Danuta:

I just wanted to tell you that I finally talked to a teacher about my problem. I talk to this teacher every Thursday now, and she has been a big help to me in dealing with my feelings.

Thanks a lot for your letter! It gave me the push I needed to really do something to get this problem solved.

What can I do about my dad?

Dear Danuta:
1. *I want you to pray for my dad.*
2. *He doesn't live with me and isn't a Christian.*
3. *Will you please pray for him.*
4. *Thank you.*
5. *I love you.*
   The End.
> Love,
> Wendy

Dear Wendy:

I'm sorry to hear that your dad doesn't live with you. I'm also sorry that he doesn't know the Lord Jesus.

But you are doing the right thing when you pray for him. Jesus loves listening to your prayers. He loves you and He wants to make you happy. He loves your dad too, and wants to live in his heart.

Your prayers will make a difference in your dad's life. It's really important that you don't stop praying even if you don't see any changes yet. Sometimes we have to believe even if we don't see any results.

You sound like a very beautiful little girl. I think you are very special to Jesus, and He wants you to know that He listens to your prayers. Expect big things to happen. Expect a miracle and remember who made the miracle happen! And remember Jesus is always with you, *no matter what.*

Dear Danuta:

I have two sons, Mike, age thirteen, and Tommy, age nine. My husband left us last year. He keeps telling us that he won't come back, but all we say is that we love him and we do.

My husband doesn't know the Lord. My sons and I pray for him because he has a drinking problem. Please pray for the Lord to touch him. The three of us do miss him so.

P.S. I just received Mike's report card. His grades are all bad. He's not trying at all.

Dear Three of Us:

My heart really goes out to you in your need and in the pain of separation from your husband and father. A family that has become divided suffers because God's love is not understood. It is a terrible waste of joy.

What is needed here is tremendous, unifying, relentless, aggressive, unceasing prayer. Pray with all your heart, together and often, that your father and husband will enter into the Kingdom of God and that Christ will come into his life. After you request that from the Lord, then the rest of your prayer should be thanks that prayer has been heard. Believe that the answer is on its way.

So many times when we pray, God answers us in the secret, spiritual world that we cannot see with our eyes. That answer then begins to appear in the natural world when every circumstance that the Lord wants worked out is in place. Don't believe that just because you don't see the answer today, it hasn't already been given to you. In fact, God knows the desires of your heart even without your telling Him! But sometimes, He wants us to acknowledge Him so that when we do get what we pray for, we know whom to thank!

I guarantee that Jesus has heard your prayers ... keep on praying and expect a change any second.

P.S. to Mike: Don't blow it ... pick up those grades ... it could mean the difference between a good life and a bad one.

Dear Danuta:

I am forty-one years old. When I was a child, my father molested me. My mom doesn't know and I need God's wisdom in how to handle this. My father and I have never been able to communicate. Do I go to him and confront him or just plain forget it? This has been on my mind for years. I want to operate in the forgiveness of the Lord.

Dear Wanting to Forgive:

I have read your letter with amazement and with gratitude to God for sustaining you and for keeping you stable through all you have been subjected to. I admire and applaud your attitude and desire to be forgiving. I join with you in believing that this shall come to pass.

I believe that with the preparation of prayer you can approach your father honestly, speaking the truth in love—stating that you want to establish forgiveness for the past between you and to develop an open, right relationship from here on. He may object out of embarrassment, but gently persevere. The Lord is on your side. The truth will set him free. Speak the truth in love. Love never fails. Love covers sin. This is all spiritually correct and it will work!

The Lord knows the sweetness of your heart and He loves you.

What can I do about my child?

Dear Danuta:

I don't know what to do about my son, who is nineteen years old. He has been going through real rebellion—drugs, profanity—and is completely out of control. He is also learning disabled, and has had a hard time in school.

Last Saturday morning, he was arrested for breaking into a house. We have not bailed him out but made him stay in jail. We've continued to pray for him and assure him of our love. But we've also made it plain that he must pay the consequences of doing wrong. What I am concerned about is his anger, bitterness, and hatred for the law. My husband and I have turned all of our problems with our son over to the Lord, realizing we can't change him ourselves.

Dear Can't Change Him Ourselves:

Your letter really makes me feel your loving concern, frustration, and dismay over your son. The Scriptures state that we are not to be anxious for long about anything. Instead, we are to handle any problem by giving thanks to God (even for the problem) and by earnestly praying to Him in the name of Jesus Christ, our advocate with the Father. And we are to entreat Him by letting Him know in detail our requests for help. Then the peace of God will take over our minds and hearts through Christ Jesus.

Study carefully and *do*: Mark 11:25

1 Thessalonians 5:16–18

Philippians 4:4–8

These are keys to release your son into God's care so He is free to act in your son's life—and to release you from the merry-go-round of effort and worry into confidence in God's capability.

Nothing, absolutely nothing is impossible with God. God wants to give you the desires of your heart. Your job is then to relax and believe that God will do it. Study Luke 18:27, Psalms 37:4, and John 6:29.

My prayers now are for your son's salvation from the complications of rebellion, drugs, anger, and hurt. Let's pray that your son will become the kind of man God wants him to be.

Dear Danuta:

My son joined the Hare Krishna movement right after college and has been with these people almost ten years. Over the years, we've kept in touch. At one point, we even "kidnapped" him, but he went back after a few months.

Needless to say, I've prayed daily that God will open my son's eyes to the truth. Now he says he wants to come home to visit for a month or so. Of course we're delighted, but very apprehensive, too. Every time he came home for two or three days in the past, we were all so tense and nervous. Please pray not only that my son will see the truth but that God will guide my husband and me as to how to deal with this visit.

Dear Tense and Nervous:

My first reaction to the news about your son's visit is that it's the best thing that could happen to him at this time. This could be the answer to your prayers.

It's very important that you relax and give your son to God. Make it as easy on yourself as you can and as hard on God as you can. With that in mind, there's no need to feel tense and nervous.

Be yourselves. Don't push your son. Actions speak louder than words.

Chapter 6 of Ephesians tells us that when we've done all that we can do, then what we must do is to stand. Stand firm . . . with the full armor of God. You have prayed. Now let God do the work. Show your son that you love him. Unconditionally. Christ will do the rest.

Dear Danuta:

I'm writing to you because you are a great one for asking point-blank questions. You truly are seeking to know God's mysteries as much as the rest of us. You don't have all the answers, admit to it freely, and I love you for it!

My mystery hinges around the life of our precious little girl. Because we are unable to have children of our own, we adopted Jenny. We know without a doubt that Jenny is our little "Moses in the bulrushes." Yet the four years we have had her have been filled with constant strife because of the emotional, mental, and physical problems that Jenny suffers. We give our all to this little girl, but the positive feedback is so slow in coming to us.

My husband and I love life. We're not bitter people, but these circumstances are draining us of our energy. We've dedicated Jenny to the Lord and committed the raising of her to God. She's been anointed with oil. But why does He let some children suffer, yet heal the slightest hurt in other children?

Dear Drained:

I have read your letter several times, and our dear Lord has quite directly led me to Psalms 89:20-34 for Jenny and for you. It begins, "I have found My servant David; With My holy oil I have

69

anointed him . . . ." The rest of the verses are promises that God has given your child. Take these promises to heart.

And when you catch your breath, read Psalms 91:14–16. "Because he has set his love upon Me, therefore I will deliver him; I will set him on high, because he has known My name. He shall call upon Me, and I will answer him; I will be with him in trouble; I will deliver him and honor him. With long life I will satisfy him, and show him My salvation."

God has Jenny and your whole family in the palm of His hand. Your only responsibility is to remain under His care. There should be no reason for all your energy to be drained in solving Jenny's problems. If she is in God's hands, it's God's energy that will help her, not yours. Hold on to His promises, no matter how long it takes.

You are blessed.

Why has my family forsaken me?

Dear Danuta:

I am sixty-two years old and my family doesn't want me. I have been on the street for six months with no place to live. It is so very hard to see even a ray of light out of this pit. My clothes are shabby, my hair is now thin. My family doesn't even care. There is nothing I can do about my situation but hang my head. Three times the police harassed me. I am so confused.

I wasn't meant to live like this. My family had affluence. We all had beautiful homes. No one lived in poverty. I am so ashamed. No wonder my family doesn't want me. I don't want me either. I have never been so low in all my life.

America should not ignore its homeless people. The acknowledgement of just one person who really cares would mean so much.

Dear Homeless:

I am distressed to hear of your condition. I will do all I can to help you out of it.

First, I've sent you the telephone number and address of the nearest Operation Blessing Center. People there are in the *business* of caring and helping. When you see them, show them this letter.

Second, let me assure you that there is love all around you, but your current situation is generating much anger. That anger can build barriers around you, preventing attempts to touch you *with* love. If the help offered is not sufficient, you have every right to say so, and continue to seek the special touch you need. At the same time, accept what is offered you in the spirit in which it was given.

Third, you will find *tremendous* relief and a dramatic change in your heart if you will reach out and help someone else. I am convinced that in the act of giving, one is automatically put on the *receiving* end of life. For instance, do you see how Mother Teresa is blessed by her work with the dying in Calcutta?

And finally, seek the face of Jesus Christ. Read His Word. He can be your best friend, companion, and hope in the midst of despair. Trust Him.

Why can't we agree about sex?

Dear Danuta:

I am thirty-six years old and have three children. I lived with a man for seven years after my divorce. When we parted, I knew that I was unhappy because I had been living in sin. Well, I am living with another man and I am still unhappy because I know that this isn't what God wants me to do. My boyfriend and I disagree about whether sex outside of marriage is sinful. I know that all these years have been lost to me because my heart told me one thing, and yet I allowed sex to be my stumbling block.

Please help me to take my stand so that I may lift this burden that has troubled my heart for years.

Dear Troubled Heart:

You are absolutely right; you cannot draw closer to God and consciously be living in sin at the same time.

Many times people ask, "How can we love God? How can we prove to God that we love Him?" The only way for us to prove that we love God is to do what He asks of us. If we love Him, we must obey Him.

And there are some tremendous consequences in obeying God. First, you may find your relationship with your boyfriend taking on a deeper dimension, one in which there is caring, compassion, and unselfishness. With sex put aside, you will see what the relationship really means to you both. Second, if you do decide to marry, having weathered the obedience to God, your next marriage will take on a new perspective. It will be clean and honorable. Third, if the relationship does not weather your obedience to God, you will have the opportunity to find one that does honor Him.

You have everything to gain by standing firm, and nothing to lose.

Stop living in sin; obey God's laws and learn to live a holy life.

Dear Danuta:

My husband had sexual intercourse with lots of women before we married, especially during his time in the service. I had no other man before him. We now have two children, a one-year-old and an infant. It is hard for me to do things now that I have the children. Consequently, there is a lot of stress at home in between the good times.

The problem is that I'm not enough for him anymore. He enjoys watching television shows with nude or nearly nude women. And he likes to go to the parks to watch girls.

It seems that during my last pregnancy, we lost something between us. That must be why he has to look elsewhere. I try to do what I can to keep a clean house and to put good meals on the table.

I've prayed to God for patience and sleep (with the kids, I don't get much sleep).

Dear Clean House:

Your sensitive letter has a lot of pain in it.

Sometimes men respond to pressure the way you describe your husband. To suddenly have to deal with two little ones as well as support a family can be very stressful for a man. You need to be able to talk candidly with him. And if you can't, you need a mediator, someone you both know and respect who loves the Lord and who can help you communicate with each other.

Or you can seek a professional counselor. You could encourage your husband to seek counseling by telling him that your happiness and your marriage depend on it.

You also need to relax. The burden of two little ones can drive anyone crazy. You and your husband need to get some time away alone together. You need time just for the two of you, even if it's just for one day. And if you can't make it for one day, try to take a walk together. It sounds as if you and your husband need a change of pace all around—and that means spiritually as well as physically. You do not mention if your husband knows the Lord. By his actions, I would think he doesn't. Persuade him—gently— to start going to church with you and the children. If that doesn't work right away, don't give up. The Bible says a wife can change her husband, not by nagging, but by setting a quiet example. You may even think of having a pastor visit your husband to talk about the Lord.

Find some help with your two babies. You might think of starting a support group of other moms in the same frenzied situation—who can share some of the burden some of the time.

Spend some time alone with the Lord every day, maybe when the babies are napping. Peace inside can help bring peace outside.

Should I marry him?

Dear Danuta:

I am in love with Jim, but he is taking so long in deciding to marry me. Recently he was laid off from his job. I feel that if he is able to get a job and stay working, he may get closer to me.

Please pray that the Lord will make Jim love me and show us the way to a marriage. Please pray too that this will be a good marriage.

Dear In Love:

How you yearn to have marriage and security! I believe this is what most people cry out in their hearts for. You have chosen Jim to be your husband, but he has not yet chosen you. God knows your heart and He knows the end from the beginning of your life. He has a plan for you. Relax, *knowing* that He has, and that in His time He *will* work things out for you. *Wait upon the Lord.* Trust Him. Resist forcing anything—especially engagement and marriage. We can make mistakes that way. So have patience. *Wait upon the Lord.* A man needs to be free to make up his own mind. Women tend to be too eager and impatient in this.

Know that the Lord will in *His time* work everything for good. If *you seek first* the Kingdom of God, everything you need *will* be given to you. He wants to give you the desires of your heart and an abundant life! So relax and trust Him to make your life beautiful. There is even the possibility that Jim is not the husband God has in mind for you—and that He has a more suitable man for you.

You can be sure that God will provide. He is faithful. You be faithful to Him, too. The following Scriptures may be helpful to you: Matthew 6:33, Philippians 4:19, and Romans 8:28.

Dear Danuta:

I'm a fifty-five-year-old widow, and I'm ready to remarry somebody really special. But I don't know if I can just *wait* and be *sure*. What are your thoughts about the man across the street, a retired policeman? His wife died eight years ago. He *used* to drink a lot but no longer does. He is seventy-six and in quite good health, and is an *enormous* help to me. We get along quite well. I have had friends say to me, "Well, when you get to be your age you can't be too picky because there's not that much to choose from!"

But something inside me keeps wanting me to wait for *better*— that makes sense to *me,* does it to *you?*

Do you think I'm doing right or should I marry someone I really like? I keep hearing you say, "Lord, you've got to start a *fire* here," and I'm like you—I want to feel "that way" about a man. After all, I'm only going this way once too, and the road's a-gettin' shorter! What do you think? Am I stubborn? Remember that popular song—"Oh, it's sad to belong to someone else when the right one comes along"? I wouldn't want to have to sing that. *Please* pray with me about all this!

Dear Ready to Remarry:

I feel that it is urgent that I write to you about that nice retired widowed policeman across the street. I've known some men in their late seventies and early eighties, and they can be pretty chipper! In fact, a seventy-eight-year-old retired vice-admiral once wanted to marry me! And I thought about it. But like you, something inside of me kept saying the real Mr. Right might be just around the corner. Besides, ten years from now, he won't be so chipper and you'll be ten years older. . . .

Why settle for anything in life if it's not the best? Do you believe that God wants a second-rate life for you just because you're fifty-five? Now, I'm not implying that the widowed policeman across the street is second-rate—but if that's what *you* think you'll never be happy about marrying him. Put this before the Lord and ask Him for a sign. You never know, the love of your life just might move next door!

None of this means a hill of beans if you really love him and the Lord has given you peace with your question. But if you don't, you're in for a lot of trouble. It seems to me you already know the answer to this.

———————

Why can't I
have another baby?

Dear Danuta:

My husband and I have been wanting a child for three and a half years. I already have four children and I pray for a child, whether it comes from adoption or from my own body.

We have been checking into some adoption agencies here in our city. One shattered our dream last year when they turned us down. They led us to believe we could adopt even though we are on welfare. My husband has been out of work for almost two years now. He has only factory skills and knows some carpentry. Please pray that my husband finds a job and that he will be saved. He is a sweet man, but needs help when he drinks. Please pray that I will soon hold a baby in my arms.

Dear Wanting a Child:

I believe it would be a mistake at this time for you to adopt a child. You will be bringing an innocent little one into an unstable home environment, which is what you have outlined to me. You have four children already whom you are not supporting well; your husband has not held a job for two years. He is not a Christian. He drinks and your only support is welfare.

You have your hands full already with four children. If you have time and energy for another child—you have time and energy to get a job yourself. It is wrong to expect government welfare for yet another child.

I do join with you now in praying for you and your husband to have a Christian marriage and home in which to teach the Word to the four children you already have. I do join with you in asking the Lord to help your husband find a good job commensurate with his capabilities, as well as a job for you, in your home, perhaps, that will help to provide for your family's needs.

You need to thank God for the children you have and to follow the Word in raising them so they will be upright, able people. Be satisfied with the children you already have. Start providing for the family you already have. Do not teach your children to live on welfare. Often welfare produces dependency, excuses, and laziness. Don't let this happen to you. You sound like a warm and loving woman with much love to share—shower it on your family, dear one.

Dear Danuta:

I need help—very fast. I'm twenty-eight years old and married. I've been out of work for two years. I prayed a lot about it and God finally gave me this job. This is my fourth week and everything is great.

I've been pregnant about four times now. I lost each baby by the time I was four months along. I was told I need a stitch around my cervix to help me hold the baby for nine months. I'm pregnant again and will be getting my stitch in two weeks.

My doctors say I need to rest and that I should quit my job. My husband has been very patient, but he's more upset than I am each time I lose our baby. I don't want to go through the loss again, and yet I don't want to lose my new job. We need the two incomes.

I want the baby so much. I'd give up the job if I had to, but I want to keep both—the job as well as the baby. I've promised God that I'll give one-tenth of my paycheck for one year if He lets me keep the job and have a beautiful baby.

Dear Wanting Both:

You not only need prayer, you need common sense, too. Sometimes we can't see the forest for the trees. I hope I can lend you some perspective, because you're much too close to your problem to see it clearly.

You say you want this baby more than anything else in the world. The doctors say you will lose the baby if you keep working. It seems to me that there is no problem about making a decision. If you really mean what you say, there is no choice. Wanting a baby more than anything else in the world means that you want a baby more than wanting a job.

Making a deal with God to tithe this year isn't much help. The Lord requires a tithe regardless of your deals, so you are not giving Him anything. If you really want to deal with God, place your trust in Him and watch Him work. Praise, prayer, and meditation can bring miracles.

If God has given you a child, that child is your first priority. Let God be God and do His part in supporting this gift. And rely on your husband's ability to provide for you. It is his responsibility. It's amazing how well the world works when each of us assumes our roles and responsibilities. You are wife and mother, and he is husband and provider. And God is God.

Sit down, put your feet up, and enjoy this pregnancy. Your world will not collapse because you sat down.

How do I love my children when I am so exhausted?

Dear Danuta:

I am an army wife with three young children. My husband makes good money and I work. Yet our bills never seem to get paid. My son needs shoes and I need glasses. A lot of my problems of irrational behavior and negativism surface when I am tired. Yet I am always tired, because my day begins at 5:30 and ends whenever it can.

I believe that God is helping me find what I want to do with my life. When my family moves to my husband's new station, I know God will reveal to us the best time and way for us to get there.

But I have so many questions for Him:

When should I give notice in my job so that it best suits my husband and children?

How do I choose the things of God rather than the world?

How do I train my children "up in the way that they should go?"

How do I love my children even when I am exhausted?

I don't want coddling, but I do need Jesus. Please respond with words of Scripture and encouragement.

Dear Exhausted:

I am so glad that you have written. I feel from your writing that you have a great need to practice taking some deep breaths and relaxing all your muscles. Between your job and maintaining your home and children, the impending move is apt to cause enormous stress. Recognizing this now, you can take action of a sort that will ease the buildup of tension and carry you through.

Lean heavily on the Lord. Trust Him. Believe His Word. Make it very real in your life. This can be a time of spiritual growth for you, so welcome all these changes as such. You asked for Scriptures. I feel the Lord has given me these for you:

Proverbs 3:5–7. "Trust in the Lord with all your heart, and lean not on your own understanding. In all your ways acknowledge Him and He shall direct your paths. Do not be wise in your own eyes; Fear the Lord and depart from evil."

Ephesians 3:16. ". . . He would grant you, according to the riches of His glory, to be strengthened with might through His Spirit in the inner man."

Ephesians 2:14. ". . . He Himself is our peace."

Isaiah 26:3. "You will keep him in perfect peace, Whose mind is stayed on You, Because he trusts in You."

Philippians 4:13. "I can do all things through Christ who strengthens me."

Rejoice and be glad! This is a time of closeness to the Lord and growth in the Lord for you—and so my prayer is stated in First Thessalonians 5:23: "May your whole spirit, soul and body be preserved blameless at the coming of our Lord Jesus Christ."

You must find time for yourself each day. Make this a time for meditation on the Word or a time for taking an exercise class or for a twenty-minute jog. Schedule your day with yourself as an important item on your list. A little rest goes a long way toward making you whole again.

Why not divorce?

Dear Danuta:

I was married to a man for five months and then he had an affair and abused me ad hit the cop who came to the door.

I filed for divorce at the time because he was out of the state. Now he is back and I don't want the divorce. I would rather have us in counseling. But he won't take counseling.

His health is bad. He's smoking and he's not saved. So he's worse now.

But I love him and want him saved and healthy.

Should I try to save the marriage or just go through with the divorce?

Dear Still Married:

SAVE THE MARRIAGE AND PRAY LIKE CRAZY!

Dear Danuta:

I am forty-two years old and have spent my whole life in turmoil and self-hatred.

I am Catholic and divorced. Sixteen years ago I remarried another Catholic, also divorced. I had two children at the time. My husband and I would undoubtedly part if it weren't for our own son and daughter. We love them very much and believe that a solid home environment is what every child needs.

But I can't rid myself of self-hatred. I've been such a stupid fool and made so many mistakes. All I do is scream and swear at my family. I can't forgive myself for putting my first two children through hell, and I can't believe divorce is okay when my religion and the Pope says it isn't and that I am living in sin.

My husband and I hate ourselves and each other because we have alienated ourselves from our church. We cannot receive the sacraments. I personally would like to join another church, but I lack the courage.

If somehow you can help me believe that Jesus loves me no matter what I've done and that He isn't condemning me for living with my husband and children after divorcing my first husband, I think I can pull myself out of this mess.

Dear In Turmoil:

So many times people get wrapped up in rules and regulations created for the sake of religion that they forget the spiritual reason for those rules and regulations.

If a church is making you feel alienated from God rather than united with Him, perhaps you had better find another church.

Hating yourself for the mistakes you've made in the past can only lead to total destruction. You alone cannot correct the errors of the past; you alone cannot atone for your sins. That is what Christ is for. He died so that we may live without bondage, guilt, sin, or shame. You say you feel like a fool and that you hate your life. In the eyes of a perfect God, we are all fools and we are all sinners. Not one of us escapes, but thanks to God, we have Christ, who has made us clean by His death. God loves us so much.

Jesus loved us enough to die for us. It doesn't sound as though you understand that.

The Lord wants your children raised in a home with a mother and a father. The Lord wants families to stay together. Let Him be the glue between you and your present husband. You can make this world better with His help. The Book of Psalms says, "As far as the east is from the west, So far has He removed our transgressions from us" (Psalms 103:12). If He has forgiven us, how dare we not forgive ourselves?

Read the Bible, dear one. Study it, devour it; begin with the Book of John. I think it will help you a great deal.

Dear Danuta:

I have been crying for the past two nights because a half hour of your program was cut out and a basketball game substituted. My husband watches these games every night. I hardly see him. He's retired now, but when he was working I only saw him a couple of hours each day! I don't know why our marriage lasted forty-three years!

I am seventy-one now and still remember the unhappy years of my childhood. I had no mother. She died when I was one and a half years old. Then her mother took over. I wish she hadn't. I was the black sheep. I wanted to take poison when I was about twelve. I finally left when I was eighteen. I have never experienced the embrace of a mother's arms or heard any words of encouragement. I'm so tired of disappointments. I've had so many in my life. The abundant life—where is it?

Dear Forty-three Years of Marriage:

If you were here, I'd hug you. God sees your hurting heart and He loves you so much.

Thank you for sharing your childhood hurts with me and your disappointment and dissatisfaction with your husband. Add to that the misery of your childhood and it means a lifetime of sorrow.

Jesus came to *overcome* the works of the devil (1 John 3:8) and He came to give life, an abundant life. He came to set the captives free, to heal broken hearts, to provide the oil of joy in place of mourning, and a covering of praise for your spirit of heaviness (Isaiah 61:1–3).

Are you willing to be made whole? Are you willing to submit yourself to be a disciple of Jesus Christ, study His Word, and *do* it? I promise you that if you are willing, He will be faithful to bring joy and peace, patience, love, faith, self-control, and gentleness into your life.

There are things you must do to free yourself from the past so that you can be a new creation in Christ Jesus. Are you willing? I believe you are. I believe that is why the Lord caused you to write to me. So here goes:

1. You need to be willing to give up all of your *past* and *present* righteous anger, hurts, disappointments, and let your expectations come through the Lord. Stop deciding how you think things ought to be. Stop judging your husband.

2. Begin by forgiving—*willingly* deciding to forgive everything and every person in the past. Right now. Willingly pray this prayer to the Lord from your heart: "Father, I confess I have clung to feeling hurt. I hereby give up feeling hurt. Heal me, Father. Let my mind be free from hurt past, present, and future. From this day forth I refuse to be hurt. Father, I confess I have held things against [say the names of everyone you need to forgive]. I willingly forgive them now and I ask You to create in me Your kind of love and forgiveness for each of them.

"Father, I hereby set my heart to be a disciple of Jesus Christ, to study, learn, do, and obey Your word in the Bible. I give You the right to make me the kind of woman You want me to be. This day I declare myself to be a new creation in Christ Jesus. Thank You for forgiving my sins and for helping me to really forgive everyone in my life. I do pray in the mighty name of Jesus Christ. Amen."

3. Affirm your position in Christ every day. Say, "I am a New Creation—the old me has passed away. I praise You, Jesus, and thank You for saving me from my old habit patterns of thinking,

acting, crying. You are changing my life into something really lovely and abundant. You work everything together for good. Thank You, Jesus."

4. Join, attend, seek Bible study and fellowship in a Spirit-led, Bible-believing, teaching church. God has placed His people there to be your brothers and sisters in Christ, to love you, to share with you and minister to you—and, in turn you need to reach out and do the same for others. It will set your mind on things above. The past is to be forgotten. Walk in the newness of life by putting on the new woman in Christ Jesus.

P.S. Look up Jeremiah 32:38, 39. Pray it for your marriage daily. Believe it. Claim that it is coming true for you and your husband.

Danuta:

I accepted Christ as my Savior a long time ago. But lately I am depressed and crying all the time, and there has been no answer to my prayers.

My husband lost his job recently. He thought we could begin again in another state. So I quit my job and left my family and our grown children to move with him. I didn't want to be alone without him, as I believe a wife should go with her husband.

But nothing has gone right since we've moved. We haven't found jobs or a decent place to live. I feel helpless and so alone. I didn't think I would miss my family so much. I think it was unfair for him to make us move and give up everything. I can't help thinking that all this misery is my husband's fault. Things are getting worse between us.

Dear Getting Worse:

Your letter is full of complaints and woe! If the Lord has convicted your heart with His Word, why aren't you listening?

You say you miss your family and that you left with your husband because you thought that was where your place was. If you truly believe your place is with your husband, why then are you punishing *him* for *your* decision by making life so miserable for you both?

Your situation will not improve. You will not get a job and neither will your husband, *until* you begin to live according to the will of God. You're fighting Him every step of the way. Your family IS your husband. Your children have their own families now. If you begin to support your husband and praise God that you have him, you may find out things are not as bad as they seem!

Enough with the pity party! If St. Paul had only gone to the places he liked, nothing would have been accomplished for Jesus! Start enjoying life. Go on an afternoon picnic with your husband and let him know you love him. Jesus has a way of shining through love. Who knows? Your husband just may fall madly in love with you all over again . . . and accept the Lord at the same time!

Be a woman. Be a wife. And have faith in God!

———————

He left me—
what do I do now?

Dear Danuta:

After twenty-six years of marriage, my husband left me for another woman. I thought we had a good marriage. At least I thought he loved me all these years. The fact that he could do this to me—lie and commit adultery while pretending to love me—has caused an open wound in my heart that won't heal. I used to think I was somebody. Now I feel like a nothing. I'm so helpless and alone.

He is still with her but wants me to forgive him. I am so full of hurt and bitterness that I can't even speak to him. Please tell me what to do.

Dear Wounded:

I received your very painful letter and I am utterly moved by the helplessness you feel.

It must have been very difficult for you to lose your husband to another woman after twenty-six years of marriage. You speak of the "open wound" in your heart ... and I am wondering if the wound you experience still is one of unforgiveness. It is a terribly difficult thing to forgive one who has hurt you so. Forgiveness is the first thing you must have in your heart before you can petition God for any changes. Have you forgiven your husband? Have you told him of your forgiveness? Have you honestly let go of all bitterness? This can be a formidable block to God's answering your prayers.

You are lonesome, and you are miserable. Release all your innermost pain to the Lord—ask God to forgive you and then to forgive your husband for his mistakes. Find a prayer partner in your church and pray boldly. Approach your husband and tell him of your prayers and your hopes.

But most of all—do not languish—you are a victorious warrior with the Lord; you are not a loser. Stop acting like one. Be bold! Stand on the Word of God with confidence. Don't begin to whimper when you don't see results right away. Pray the promises of Christ, not your problems. And always praise God in all things. In Him you will find your strength.

I suggest you read the Psalms for strength and courage and praise. They are wonderful! At times like these, cling to the Psalms . . . they are precious bolsters of faith; affirmations of all God's promises.

Dear Danuta:

I am going through a divorce, although I am not divorced yet. I am trying to save the marriage. I wrote my husband a letter, and he does not answer me. He lives with another girl. He says to friends that he doesn't love me.

I haven't been able to buy groceries for three months because of doctor bills. I have been in turmoil so long. I went to a credit-counseling center and they are handling my bills. I thought the Lord didn't care about me. But He does.

Got any advice?

Dear Looking for Advice:

It seems to me that you've done everything you can to save your marriage. And if you really do want your husband back, you must persevere in prayer, and I mean *persevere!* Find a prayer partner and pray that man back to his marriage commitment. Pray like you've never prayed before. Don't give up. God can do the impossible—if we would only believe.

In the end, if your husband, by his own will, chooses to disregard the signs and nudgings of God and marries another woman—let him go, with your forgiveness, and find someone who loves Jesus.

How can I help him stop drinking?

Dear Danuta:

My husband and I have been married for fifteen years. Our biggest fights are over his drinking. Once we separated and he left the state. I let him come back if he would quit drinking because I had. He came back. He didn't drink but then he backslid and things were worse than before. He is insanely jealous—doesn't want me to work. He almost choked me to death once and hit me on several occasions.

Once, I took my husband to church and he went for the rebirth. But soon the demon was back. I believe he is worth saving. Maybe this is all my fault. I don't feel sorry for myself, just confused and lost. I love my husband and don't want us to live this way, always a slave to the demon of alcohol.

Dear Confused and Lost:

I am glad you have written to me to share your deepest needs. In your letter I see things that you can do to alter your situation. I pray you will receive advice from me—all of it will help you become a true disciple of Jesus Christ.

In a situation like yours, the best advice I could ever give is that we can only change ourselves. Sometimes our own change reaches others and they change with us.

1. Find a spirit-filled, Bible-teaching church. Seek all that God has for you. You need the Baptism of the Holy Spirit. Ephesians 3:16 states, ". . . He would grant you, according to the riches of His glory, to be strengthened with might through His spirit in the inner man."

2. Locate an Al-Anon group (part of Alcoholics Anonymous), where you will learn how to deal with your alcoholic husband. They will show you that his alcoholism is not your fault. You need this conviction. You need the fellowship of believers in joining a church and the understanding you will garner from attending Al-Anon.

3. There is hope for you. Begin by refusing to speak negatively about yourself. You have been under oppression from lack of His Word. Grab onto 2 Corinthians 2:14, which states that we are *always* triumphant in Jesus Christ. Believe these words; cling to them.

I didn't see anywhere in your letter whether you and your husband pray together, or read the Word together; whether you belong to a church; whether the Lord is the Lord of your life. Any and all of these would give you more help in changing the direction of your lives. Most certainly your husband could use the peace and tenderness of Christ.

4. Ask God to draw your husband to Jesus Christ to receive salvation and deliverance from alcohol. Pray out loud. Mean it. Believe that He hears and will answer your prayer, for it is in accord with His will. He wants no one to be lost. Study 1 John 5:14, 15: Jesus came to overcome the works of the devil so your husband can be free of alcoholism and you can be free from self-condemnation and the fear of failure.

Then begin daily aloud by yourself to praise and thank God for saving your husband and setting him free from alcohol. Praise and thank Him for changing you.

Begin to claim Jeremiah 32:38, 39 for a beautiful marriage in Christ.

Study the Word, believe the Word, claim it for your life. If you will earnestly seek to study and do His Word, I guarantee your life will become beautiful.

I'm excited about what is going to happen. Be patient, though. It has taken years for you to reach where you are. It may take time for this all to work out, but I know it will. Yes! There is hope!

And for your husband, it is so important that he knows you love and support him. Sometimes love and support must be of the tough variety. Insist he seek help. Strongly encourage him to begin with Alcoholics Anonymous. Their program has breathed life back into countless thousands of people. Your husband must take the first step toward recovery. He has to get well for himself. Storm heaven with prayer for him. He may slip back from his efforts—but forgive, and stick with him through this. Alcoholism is not just his problem—it's a problem you both have and a problem you can both conquer with perseverance, prayer, and a whole lot of love. God bless you.

———————

Am I to blame
for being raped?

Dear Danuta:

When I was a teenager I was raped by a friend of the family. I was very close to his wife, and of course that ended our friendship! I've felt destroyed all these years, and am still distraught over it even though I'm now married.

I have never told anyone of the rape. No one would ever suspect this man of rape, and at the time I thought no one would believe me because my teenage years were so mixed up. I couldn't go to his wife and tell her that her husband raped me. They had two children under ten. Anyway, he told me he would deny it. I felt so ashamed and broken in spirit.

So as you can see, I have come into marriage a very insecure person. I want to quit feeling rejected and worthless and be the kind of person my husband wants, needs, loves, and enjoys.

Dear Destroyed:

How it hurt to read your letter! You poor dear; hope is all around you and all you can see is the darkness.

Some time ago I was attacked by a weirdo in a shopping mall. Fortunately, I was not hurt, and I was not raped, but the feelings are somewhat the same. I too felt ashamed, dirty, angry, and depressed . . . not to mention that my boyfriend at the time left me because he didn't believe me! It can be tough. But it doesn't have to be so.

When Jesus was so cruelly beaten and whipped with those leather strips that tore out bits of His flesh, when He was spit upon, abused, and finally nailed, naked, to a cross to die a humiliating and undeserved death—don't you know why? He bore all the torment, pain, guilt, anger, shame, fear, and humiliation for you—so you don't have to. That's why Christ died. By His stripes you are healed (*see* 1 Peter 2:24) from all that garbage that the world dishes out. If you are under condemnation for what happened to you, then you haven't really gotten the message. If you are allowing Satan to impose his filthy lies upon you, to make you feel depressed and worthless—then you haven't claimed victory through Christ.

All you have to do, dear one, is pray to Jesus. Thank Him for bearing all the pain that you feel, and ask Him to forgive you for your sins. Then accept the forgiveness. The next step is to thank Him and invite Him inside of you. He will wash all the sin and pain and guilt and shame away. It will be gone! THAT'S WHY HE DIED! Once you have accepted Jesus as I just described ... you then have the actual POWER to remove all evil and satanic influences from your life. Satan MUST obey. Rebuke the demon in the name of JESUS—Your Savior. Remember, the guilt and depression you feel IS NOT from God!

Certain things can block our channel to God. One of those things is unforgiveness or bitterness. You must forgive the man who raped you, not just verbally but in your heart. Pray for him. That unforgiveness has led to fear that is affecting not only your life, but the life of your marriage. We are told in the Lord's prayer to ask God to "forgive us our debts, as we forgive our debtors" (Matthew 6:12). Clear your heart before God and let Him take away all your bitterness and fear. As a child of God, you are totally protected by our Lord Jesus. You have nothing to be afraid of.

Psalms 37:4 says, "Delight yourself also in the Lord, And He shall give you the desires of your heart." Read the Bible, continue to pray, and believe that your prayers are answered.

Don't be afraid to talk with your husband or a counselor or an elder from the church—any good solid Christian—about your experience. They will not hate you . . . they will love you . . . as I do . . . as He does.

If God loves you enough to send His Son to suffer and die for you, do you have any right to think you're worthless? You have to *forgive yourself* for even imaginary guilt. You were not to blame.

Your husband loves you. Believe him. Accept it. God loves you. Believe Him. Accept it. See yourself through the eyes of those who love you until you get into the habit of seeing your great value to Christ and your family through your own eyes.

You are loved!

———————

Part 3

"Maybe God's mad at me . . ."

Problems in our lives are only what we choose to make of them. We have the ability to make our problems as big as mountains or as small as pebbles beneath our feet. We always have the choice as to how we react to the difficulties we encounter. We are responsible for our reactions in the world, and we are equally responsible for how we solve our problems.

We may choose to shoulder our burdens ourselves and slowly drown beneath the weight, or we may choose to hand the problems over to Jesus Christ and allow Him to work through the tough times.

The results can be dramatically different. Those who choose to carry the burdens and try to control their situations talk of suicide when they can handle no more. Others who view their difficulties as opportunities for growth and for drawing close to our Lord know peace in the face of chaos.

Why are so many bad things happening to me?

Dear Danuta:

I am forty-nine and have been ill since I was three. That is much too long for anyone. I wonder what I was born for if I'm constantly sick and in pain all the time.

I have a congested heart, weight problems, tumors and sores on my arms and legs. I also have thyroid problems and am greatly afraid of cancer of the thyroid returning. I am a very nervous person on top of everything.

Please help me, Danuta. I am desperate and can't take it anymore.

Dear Can't Take It:

I grieve with you for your suffering and illness. Who knows the mind of God? He has His own reasons why these tribulations come upon us.

Nowhere in your letter do I see you mention God as a source of comfort or love. Your agony is all important to you. But the Bible tells us that God has to come first—that we must love Him with our whole mind and whole spirit and whole heart.

Job, who suffered greatly, did love God. One such evidence is the statement, "Now acquaint yourself with Him and be at peace. Thereby good will come to you" (Job 22:21). Read Job, chapters 30 through 40, where God reveals some of the mysteries of His own mind in answering Job's questions about suffering. I can only console you with the Word of God Himself. May these verses be a refreshment and a revelation to you. Do not be angry with God; just love Him. Your world could change.

Dear Danuta:

I am a sixty-five-year-old widow. I do not know what is wrong with me. It seems impossible for one person to have so many problems.

I broke my leg five years ago and have had two bone transplants and plastic surgery. I am in constant pain. I stayed in bed fourteen months and almost starved. No friends came to help.

Finally, I forced myself to get up and got a job helping an elderly lady in a wheelchair. I worked a year, then started bleeding internally and wound up in the hospital with cancer of the colon. I am now taking chemotherapy.

Two weeks ago, my car was wrecked. Now I don't have a way to look for work or go to church. I called my pastor and he said he would have someone pick me up for services. I got dressed and am still waiting. No one came.

Danuta, why are so many bad things happening to me? I try to be a good person, but things just get worse. Maybe God's not listening at all.

Dear Trying:

You are still a young and vital woman. May I encourage you to reach out to *help* others; yes, while *you* are in need. Perhaps you sew—you could help organize activities over the phone for church . . . you could find some helpful way to get involved again with life.

Phone your pastor back and remind him that you need a ride to church and elsewhere.

Often things can become complicated and beyond our understanding—beyond our ability to handle and change them in the natural world. As humans, we tend to concentrate on what is wrong and try to work it out ourselves. And we get angry and confused when we cannot make things right.

But as we walk with Jesus in the yoke of discipleship, He bears our burdens with us. We put our trust in Him and in His guidance as we walk together. It is no longer necessary for us to figure things out for ourselves. We walk by faith not by sight (2 Corinthians 5:7), and we walk not after the flesh but after the Spirit (Romans 8:1).

As we walk together, He opens some doors and closes others. With Him comes a very real sense of peace and joy. Often we are guided by His Word—Scripture—which is a lamp unto our feet showing us the way (Psalms 119:105). Being a Christian means believing in, trusting in, and relying on Jesus, with whom we are joint heirs to all that God has for us.

Stop concentrating on *your problems*—look at the promises of Christ. Have a joyous outlook, reach others in spite of your own pain. A change in attitude can make a remarkable difference in your life.

Through this new approach to life, you may find that God wanted to get your attention—to draw you to Him so that He could love you beyond your capacity to hold so much love. Sometimes it is only when we are totally broken down with no one else to turn to and nowhere else to go that our eyes *finally* see the One who does care and who does love us.

Have you reached that point? Does He have your full attention? Are you ready to rest *completely* in Him?

Watch what happens now!

Why did my loved one have to die?

Dear Danuta:

I recently lost my grandson in a fatal accident. The death has devastated us all. My daughter has been wonderful in this sad time. But she no longer has her only son on this earth.

Is it right for someone to die so young? Is this part of a pattern, a plan and not a punishment? Where does God fit in? Please recommend something to read about death.

Dear Bereaved Grandmother:

For me to sit smugly behind a desk many miles away from you and rattle off some glib answer as to why this happened would be presumptuous beyond measure. There is no way I can honestly say that I know why this happened to your loved one. Furthermore, I seriously doubt if there is any single individual who can adequately explain the reason for this death.

The Apostle Paul, however, was able to bless "the Father of our Lord Jesus Christ, the Father of mercies, and God of all comfort; who comforts us in all our tribulation, that we may be able to comfort those who are in any trouble, with the comfort with which we ourselves are comforted by God." He was able to say this even when he had been "burdened beyond measure, above strength, so that we despaired even of life" (2 Corinthians 1:3, 4, 8).

The Bible says that God will not go off and leave us alone in our time of need, that He will not put more on us than we can bear, but will also show us how to escape despair. Unfortunately, tragedies do happen. I talked to a fifteen-year-old boy just recently who came in on crutches and one leg, because cancer had cost him his other leg. He was taking chemotherapy treatments with no assurance of cure. "Unfair," was the cry that welled up out of his spirit; unfair for young people in the prime of life to be cut off; unfair for children who have not had a chance to live to be taken away; unfair for good people to perish while the evil prosper. Unfair—unfair! Jesus never promised that life would always be fair, but He did promise that you could be victorious over the circumstances in which you found yourself.

Jesus used the illustration of the man who built his house on sand and the man who built his house on rock. The same circumstances—winds, rains, and flood—beat upon both houses. One fell, whereas one stood firm because it was built on rock. (*See* Matthew 7:24–27.) While we cannot be responsible for adversity or the circumstances that overwhelm us, we alone are responsible for our attitude toward these circumstances. And it is God's hope that we will see in the worst tragedies His ability to work everything for our good (Romans 8:28).

I recommend a book to you written by Eleanor T. Mead. The book was published by Logos International in 1977 and is called *Lay Up Your Treasures in Heaven.* While the only one who can truly comfort you at a time like this is Jesus Christ, those who have experienced tragedy can give you insight into God's power in desperate times. May the Lord bless you richly and cause His face to shine upon you and give you peace, while you remember that God gave up *His* only Son so that none should taste death— not even your departed grandson—but only eternity.

───────

I'm afraid to die—who can help?

Dear Danuta:

I am a twenty-nine-year-old housewife and mother with two small daughters. I am dying of cancer discovered on the day I was taking my second child home from the hospital.

I know many people who have cancer have given themselves to God for healing and the cancer is leaving them. I want so much to do that too. Yet I have an enormous wall of fear that is keeping me from turning myself over. I'm so afraid of dying and leaving my girls motherless. I need your prayers and guidance. I have turned to your counselors on the free line; yet it seems that no matter what I do, the cancer stays with me. I'm running out of time—I need a miracle.

Dear Wall of Fear:

Your letter really touches my heart and I am glad you wrote because I want you to know we have a wonderful heavenly Father who loves you. *Nothing* is impossible with Him. Nothing (Luke 1:37 and 18:27). With God all things are possible (Matthew 19:26, Mark 10:27).

You have your part to carry out. Jesus said that if any man would come after Him, he must deny himself and pick up his cross and follow Him. (*See* Matthew 16:24.) That means denying yourself the right to self-pity.

Matthew 13:57, 58 tells us that Jesus could not perform a miracle in the midst of unbelief. Your "wall of fear" and lack of faith are preventing this miracle from happening.

What are you more afraid of, losing your cancer or losing your life? If I were to offer you a chance for complete healing, a total loss of your cancer, what is it that you would be afraid of? Fear has a way of making us hold on to things. Fear is like glue to our problems; without it we could step back from the problem and view it objectively and unemotionally. You need something to dissolve the glue. That something is love. Perfect love dissolves fear and perfect love comes from Christ unconditionally.

Fear is a trick of the devil and is one of the ways he controls man. Fear can be overcome by using Scripture: studying, believing, declaring, personalizing specific Scriptures in prayer. Once is not enough. These Scriptures must become real to you and stated over and over. Study, believe, and declare the following to overcome fear: Deuteronomy 31:8, Psalms 23:4, Psalms 34:4, Proverbs 18:10, Isaiah 41:10, Matthew 28:20, 2 Thessalonians 3:3, 2 Timothy 1:7.

Healing can be withheld by lack of forgiveness. Those who do study, use, and do His Word are as excited as I am about what God can and will do in our lives!

Cleave to Christ with the same passion with which you have been cleaving to your problems. Take your eyes off the cancer and cast them on Jesus. Throw yourself on Him. Abandon yourself to Him. Let go of everything. Let go of your children. Let go of your husband. Let go of your cancer. Let go of yourself. Only then can Christ work through your faith. Then fear will never take hold of you again.

Am I wasting my time with God?

Dear Danuta:

I've had it! I've put away my Bible, and I'm not praying anymore. The more I pray, the worse things get. Now don't tell me God loves me. You don't keep hurting someone you love. God is mad at me and He's turned away. And I'm wasting my time trying to change God's curse into a blessing.

But I thought I'd make one last try. *You* pray for me. He's not listening to me. Maybe He'll listen to you.

I've prayed for Him to find me a husband, but I'm still very, very single.

Dear Wasting:

Boy, do you sound angry and bitter!

Sometimes we tend to blame God for not coming through on things that He never promised to give us in the first place! Naturally, He wants us to be happy. He wants us to have joy in our lives. But are we always sure what is best for us from moment to moment? Have you asked God for direction in your needs, or have you simply supplied Him with a shopping list as though you were writing to Santa Claus?

How could God deliver to you a perfect mate if you are hurt and angry? Even if the right guy DID come along, do you think he'd love your bitterness? Wouldn't it be more like God to help you grow into an ideal mate before putting you with someone?

Wouldn't it be a more perfect plan if God wanted to make you a whole, joyful, trusting woman first, before He gave you the responsibility of supporting another human being's needs?

It sounds like you're putting very definite limits on God's ability to work with you. It seems that you have established a time limit by somehow making deadlines for Him or else! Have you limited HOW you want God to work in your life?

It's time to exercise your faith. Trust that God has the best intentions in the world for you. Have faith that no matter what, God will show you something valuable out of all the difficult times. Abandon yourself to Him; do it with love; read the Bible to know what He wants for you; surround yourself with mature Christian friends who can help counsel you. Go to church and pray with others. Reach out to help others who are in need. Soon you will find yourself more concerned for them than for yourself. You will find yourself free.

Being angry with God won't hurt Him . . . but it could cause you great harm. If you really mean business, follow my advice.

Dear Danuta:

I have no luck praying to the Lord. In fact, I think the Bible is like Aesop's Fables. Nobody I know has ever been healed by the Lord. And the healing done by the "700 Club" I think is for the birds. My motto is wine, women, and song.

I read a lot of occult books. I have faith in witchcraft and voodoo and I believe that people from other worlds outside our galaxy came down to earth to live.

But I still don't believe in the Bible. What can I do to get faith? I want so much to be Christian. I am sixty-six years old.

Dear Wine, Women, and Song:

I get the very strong impression that your opinions are not formed through facts. For a sophisticated gentleman, you seem to be caught up in something you say you don't believe in. That leads me to believe that there is something inside of you that needs to know the truth. Sixty-six years is a long time to live without it.

You say that you read a lot of occult books and have faith in voodoo. Have you read the Bible with the same intensity? Now don't get me wrong, I believe in voodoo, too. By that I mean, I believe there are forces at work in the other kingdom. It's just a question of which kingdom you'd rather be affiliated with, the one that will save you or the one that will kill you. If you really mean business about Christianity, tell God you're sorry for your sins, turn away from those sins, quit going your own way, and doing your own thing, and abide by God's will for the remainder of your days. Seek God with your whole heart; seek His kingdom and His righteousness. If you will commit yourself to Him, making Him the Lord of your life and loving your neighbor as you love yourself, you will find the peace and fulfillment you have missed for the first sixty-six years of your life. Spend time reading the New Testament, concentrating initially on Matthew, Mark, Luke, and John. Spend time in prayer. Find a church, attend regularly, seek friendship and fellowship with folk from the church. Allow God to change your mind—be teachable and open to the Spirit of God.

Blessings to you! It is my prayer that when you do write again, you'll be a man who knows the peace that Jesus gives and will be singing God's praises.

Dear Danuta:

I don't trust many people, especially Christians. I don't really have a friend to share all this with, so I figured you wouldn't mind my writing to you.

I used to be a real good Christian, but I just couldn't stay with it when it got boring. I'm not satisfied with my life. I'm depressed a lot. I feel lonely and anxious, as if something is missing inside me.

I don't love my parents. I guess I don't love them because they not only didn't have time for me when I needed them, but my mother would hit us with whatever was handy when she got angry.

I won't blame you if you don't want to write to me. I'm not anybody special or important. But I do hope you will answer this letter yourself.

You don't appear to be bored with God (it shows in your eyes). But please don't present a boring God to me. And don't present God as a crutch. If I am right in saying that you're not bored with God—how do you keep from getting bored with Him? What keeps it exciting?

Dear Bored:

I'm answering this letter personally because you seem to be a person who is being pursued by the Hound of Heaven . . . and you don't recognize the symptoms. You have revealed so much of yourself in your letter and I think you may begin to recognize some patterns before we talk about a solution.

You say you don't trust many people, "especially Christians," but you also concede that you don't have a best friend of any denomination to share some of your deeper feelings with. It would appear that you don't trust people PERIOD, and you just happen to pick on Christians as a scapegoat for your isolation.

I think that not loving your parents and the way in which you were hurt by your mother may be the reason for your distrust of people, not Christianity. I also sense low self-esteem from your letter; you call yourself "not anybody special or important" and are willing to understand why someone would toss your letter away instead of treating it with some respect and care. This all leads up to what's going on inside of you.

Basically, I don't think you believe you are worthy to be loved.

And nothing could be further from the truth! Did you ever consider that in the eyes of God not a single one of us is worthy to be loved by Him? And yet, if you were the only person on earth, Jesus Christ would have suffered the same agony and died on that miserable cross just for you. Now that's love, my friend. That's love that you can depend on and hold on to when everything else around you looks bleak. When all else fails you . . . He will not.

If you thought living a Christian life was boring—you don't know what a Christian life is! You say you were "a real good Christian." Unfortunately, many of us are . . . we all go through the motions . . . going to church and yawning; looking at the time; not doing this or that; abiding by rules and regulations set up by man to honor a God that we don't even understand. *Now that's boring!* That's called "religion." The Christ I'm talking about is a Power, a Lover. He's ALIVE, living somewhere in the universe taking up space . . . *alive* . . . and waiting with open arms to show you just how exciting He is. But before He can show you anything, you have to be willing to see! It's like a guy who offers you ten dollars—if you don't take it, whose fault is that? The guy who is holding the money out to you? Or the hand that refuses to accept it?

I am talking about a personal relationship with Christ. He is someone who answers prayers on a regular basis and who causes the most unbelievable "coincidences" to occur on a regular basis. He heals bodies and minds and He will turn your life upside down to make all things come together for good. Jesus has made thousands of promises to us that He will not break. If there is a financial difficulty—He will send you money from an unexpected source. If there is an argument at home, He will bind a family together. If there is a need of any kind in your life—all you have to do is ask Him and He will answer the innermost desires of your heart. There is not a single person, place, or thing on this earth that can faithfully perform all these things for you other than Jesus Christ.

The neat thing about Christ is that He invites you to try Him, to prove that what He says is so. But first, you must find a church that teaches the Word of God based on the Bible. Second, you need to ask for the baptism of the Holy Spirit at that church. Third, you need to get near other Christians who are born-again to get an idea of how Christ works on a daily basis. There are many churches to choose from ... but I suggest that you find a church that is spirit-filled—you want action? You'll get it there!

You know what sounds boring to me? The life you're living. The depression that haunts you. That empty feeling. Those are symptoms of a life without God. We hear from thousands upon thousands of people who have the same problem ... and those multitudes have found incredible answers with Jesus Christ.

Ask Him to come into your heart ... and to show you what to do next. Then keep your eyes open because He will begin to open doors for you in a way that you have never imagined possible! It's guaranteed.

Let me know of your progress.

———

What good is prayer?

Dear Danuta:

Last month I decided to join the "700 Club." I will try this for one year. If I don't see a big turnaround in my life at the end of this year, then I'll just forget it.

My husband of twenty-seven years died seven years ago. I brought suit against his doctors. It took four years to come to trial. I lost the trial. I appealed and lost that. There were areas of negligence found by the judge, but they were never allowed into the evidence.

I've prayed and prayed and prayed some more. I'm beginning to think that God needs a certain number of whipping boys. Am I one? I've asked God with my mouth to forgive doctors. I can't mean it in my heart. The suffering my son and I have gone through defies description. Really, Danuta, I'm reaching up as hard as I can. It wouldn't hurt Him to reach down, would it?

Will you pray for me?

Dear Reaching Up:

It really grieves me that you are hurting so. Thank you for your letter. My heart goes out to you for the hurt and pain that you have suffered.

One of the great things about knowing Jesus Christ is that He can do for us what we can't do for ourselves or for others. All we have to do is rest in Him and have the knowledge that He wants the best for us. Do not trouble yourself. Rest instead in the love that Jesus has for you and know that your prayers are answered. That is one of the great promises of all time. Prayers are heard and answered in God's time. Just because it's not in your time, do not let that hurt you or worry you. Know that it will be heard in the Lord's time and that means that the desires of your heart will be granted.

Learn to lean on Him and not on yourself. This is the year when Jesus is calling many to His kingdom. It could be the year that He wants you to be His servant in this. Keep praying and so will I. Praise God! Romans 8:28 tells us "all things work together for good to those who love God."

Yes, I'll pray for you. Right now I have paused and I have prayed. I trust that in reading my letter, your heart will be opened to willingly receive my ministry and that you will willingly respond in action to God's Word as I have presented it to you.

That vengeance belongs to God is a fact stated in a number of Scriptures in the Old Testament and in the following verses: Deuteronomy 32:35, Psalms 99:8, Isaiah 34:8, Jeremiah 50:15, Ezekiel 24:25, 2 Thessalonians 1:6–8, Hebrews 10:30. Study these Scriptures.

That we will have tribulation in this world (because it is a world full of sin) is a fact—but, we are to be overcomers with Jesus (John 16:33).

To be an overcomer, we need not only read God's Word but do His Word (James 1:22) in order to really know its power; otherwise we err (Mark 12:24).

Jesus said if you want to come after Him you must deny yourself (Matthew 10:33) and that you are to pray for your enemies, love them, and ask God to bless them (Matthew 5:43–48).

Study these Scriptures and set your heart to do them. Deny that old self. Be renewed in the mind by cleansing God's Word (Ephesians 5:26). Then in prayer aloud to God, forgive:

"Father, I confess I have erred. I have not done Your word. I have let 'self' rule my thinking. I hereby set my heart to do Your word. I willingly act now to forgive [add names], releasing them from my judgment into Your care so You may deal with them. Vengeance is Yours, not mine. I ask that You create in my heart Your kind of forgiveness and love for each one. I ask that You bless each of these people and do good unto them. I thank You for releasing me from Your judgment. Amen."

Having done all of the above, put the past in the past and press on to God's high and wonderful calling for you (Philippians 3:13).

Thank God for your son and teach him by the forgiveness and change in your life the real values of a Christian life. Thank Him for everything (1 Thessalonians 5:16–18). You won't have to wait a year to see beautiful changes in your life. God promises!

Dear Danuta:

Recently my wife decided to leave our home. We both belong to a church, and she claims to be born-again, but I feel she fell prey to the temptations of the world. How else could she claim to be a Christian and leave her children and husband like this? She says she wants a new life and that I am holding her back. Danuta, my heart is breaking because of this. But I still want her. I am willing to wait because I believe she is making a terrible mistake. But there is no way she will listen to me.

Dear Willing to Wait:

Thank you so much for your letter . . . reading it made my heart ache. You sound so very hurt and desperate.

Obviously your dear wife is struggling with the seductions of the world and does not hear the voice of God clearly. If she truly were born-again she would not be breaking your heart or your home. Love does not hurt and tear others apart; it builds us up and fills us with selflessness. She needs the Lord. She needs His love so that it can flood over to you and your little family. There is really nothing you can do in the world to help her find Him. But you can pray!

Prayer is a powerful weapon against the Antichrist . . . against all those principalities and powers of darkness that fight against the Light of Jesus. (*See* Ephesians 6:12.) Prayer is a miracle in action. We have thousands of examples at the "700 Club" of lives transformed through prayer. You must pray, in the name of Jesus, that she be reconciled to your family and that the scales from her eyes be lifted. You must take authority over the influences around her—in the name of Jesus—and cast them from her. You're the head of the family; take charge! Be bold and demand in prayer that Satan leave and that she return to you.

Since you are fortunate to have a church, petition some prayer partners to pray with you. (There is so much force when two or more gather in His name!) Give her up to Him and pray constantly for her. Remember, too, that despair on your part is not from God, but from Satan. Have faith, my friend, that the Lord is faithful. He will not let you down. Do not let Satan claim his slimy victory over your hopeful heart.

I also recommend that you listen to the needs of your wife. Are you encouraging her to be the best she can be? Are you nurturing her and loving her as Christ loves us? What can you do to change?

I recommend the Psalms when you feel low. David wrote them when he got himself in all sorts of trouble . . . and they are food for a sad soul!

Dear Danuta:

I have prayed, cried, and worried for a very long time about my family. By this, I mean my parents, my sister, and my brother. My mother is full of bitterness and hate. She wants nothing to do with God because she wants to get revenge on people who have hurt her in the past. She trusts in horoscopes.

My daddy is quiet and sweet. But he is so sad and feels so useless now that he is retired. My sister has never been married and lives at home. A year ago she was fired from her job and she can't seem to find another one. My brother is mentally retarded. He needs healing and wants to know about God but my mother does not want me talking about Jesus and the Bible.

I want to pray for them before I leave their house. But I am afraid they will get mad at me. I sense that my family's salvation is an urgent matter. Please pray for my family.

Dear Talking About Jesus:

Have received your heartfelt letter regarding your longtime prayers for your family's salvation. Hang on—keep thanking and praising God for each of your loved one's salvation and life change.

You may use some effectual prayers to hasten the outcome. Use Matthew 12:29 and Matthew 18:18, 19 to bind Satan's control over each of your family members. ". . . How can one enter a strong man's house and plunder his goods, unless he first binds the strong man? . . . Whatever you bind on earth will be bound in heaven, and whatever you loose on earth will be loosed in heaven . . . if two of you agree on earth concerning anything that they ask, it will be done for them by My Father in heaven." Then ask God to draw each one to Jesus according to John 6:44. The Lord wants you to know the Scripture and use its power, so that by speaking His Word you will overcome the devil as Jesus did (1 John 3:8).

God sends His Word to heal your brother (Psalms 107:20). It is for you to speak and decree. Mark 11:22–25 has miraculous teaching on praying and believing what you've stated in prayer.

I'm excited about what's happening in your family and about how God is using you. Do not waver. Hang on faithfully, no matter how long it takes. God is faithful. All your hopes for your family shall come to pass.

Can God heal me?

Dear Danuta:

I live by myself and it's kind of hard as I am not from this area and the people don't care for outsiders. I ask your prayers for myself as I have a hernia and a burning in my throat.

Do you think God can heal me?

Dear By Myself:

Thank you for writing to me. I pray now as I write that these words of encouragement will increase your faith and will result in your taking some action to bring about needed changes in your situation.

You state that you live alone and people around you seem not to welcome strangers. That can change. You reap what you sow. Expect good things to happen. Get all excited; God wants you to prosper and have an abundant life. Don't confess negatives. Ask God to give you favor with your neighbors. Show forth loving concern to your neighbors. Do all in the Lord's name. Ask God to give you Christian friends to love, enjoy, and spend time with. Sow love—and you will reap abundantly.

About your hernia and the burning in your throat . . . do you belong to a Bible-believing, full gospel church? You need to belong to such a church. Ask the elders to lay hands on you and anoint you with oil for healing.

These verses may help: "Is anyone among you sick? Let him call for the elders of the church, and let them pray over him, anointing him with oil in the name of the Lord. And the prayer of faith will save the sick, and the Lord will raise him up. And if he has committed sins, he will be forgiven" (James 5:14, 15). "For with God nothing will be impossible" (Luke 1:37 and 18:27). Nothing.

Dear Danuta:

This is a preliminary praise report giving God the credit for an expected healing. I believe that it will help my family's and my faith to grow if I express openly what God has done, is doing, and will continue to do.

Last Thanksgiving Day, my sister fell and broke her neck. Her condition was so critical that the emergency room doctors told us she would not survive the night.

My sister did survive but was totally paralyzed.

Three months after the accident, you said, "There is somebody who has a broken neck and is paralyzed from the neck down. The paralysis will fade and you will be restored to a full life again."

When I heard that, I experienced a great feeling of elation, spiritually and emotionally. I knew the Holy Spirit meant this healing for my sister.

The brace she wore for several months soon will be replaced by a collar. Now we are seeing a little movement in her left arm and right leg. Perhaps this healing will be gradual.

I am praying that my sister's healing will bring her unsaved family and friends to the knowledge of the Lord.

Dear Praying:

I've received your letter. I am so glad you wrote and I praise God for your faith in His healing for your sister.

I've known of two specific and recent cases of miraculous healing taking place after doctors had stated that medically nothing further could be done. Family members, full of faith, determinedly took turns reading healing Scriptures to the patient.

They personalized the Scriptures by inserting the patient's name in appropriate places.

You can do this for your sister. The following are some suggested healing Scriptures you could use, claiming and declaring them to be true for your sister. Psalms 107:2 states, "Let the redeemed of the Lord say so." Job 22:28 states, "You will also declare a thing, and it will be established for you." Hosea 14:2a says, "Take words with you, and return to the Lord." In Isaiah 43:26 He says, "Put me in remembrance (of my word)." Jesus used Scripture to overcome Satan. He said, "It is written ..." and quoted Scriptures. There's tremendous power in the Word.

Psalms 9:9, 30:2, 34:10b, 34:19, 55:18, 94:19, 97:10b, 103:3, 116:8–10, 119:93, 145:14; Isaiah 40:29, 50:7, 53:4a, 53:5; Jeremiah 30:17; Proverbs 16:3; John 8:36; Matthew 8:17b, 15:28b; Romans 8:2, 8:32; 1 Corinthians 2:5, 2:16; 2 Corinthians 2:14a, 5:7; 1 John 3:8b; 3 John 2; 1 Peter 2:24; Hebrews 4:12.

May God show forth His mercy and His grace!

———————

What can I do
to make Him love me?

Dear Danuta:

So many things have been happening to me. First, my father died of a heart attack; then I got married and divorced. My best friend died and I lost my job. My roommate's father gave me a job, but now his store is failing. As you can see, I've lost my faith in God. I even tried to kill myself, but I failed at that, too.

I'm not a bad person. People tell me I have a heart of gold. But I feel that the Lord isn't interested in me.

What can I do to make Him love me? Is He putting my faith to the test? If so, I'm no good at praying. He never answers me. How do I go about being born again and starting a rewarding life? Please show me the way to be happy and fulfilled.

Dear Show Me:

You asked me what you can do to make Jesus love you. You don't have to do anything. There's nothing you could do to force Jesus to love you. He loves you unconditionally. That's the purest kind of love there is.

But we might ask—how do you love God? You love God by obeying Him. And to learn how to obey Him we have to read His book, the Bible. The most wonderful things happen when you do that. Your life takes on a whole new dimension. You begin to live the "rewarding life" you are looking for.

Find a church that teaches the love of Christ. Find a prayer partner. Learn to pray. Look for opportunities to help others. In loving others, you will see the face of Christ. God uses people to help people. Maybe you and your roommate could become prayer warriors together. Pray for your store together. You need action in your life, girl, and there's no greater adventure than loving God. All sorts of crazy, wonderful things happen when you do. But your first step is finding a spirit-filled church and spending time with people who understand this wonderful adventure.

You said in your letter that you felt your faith was being put to the test . . . maybe it is! So many times I have faced enormous difficulties with no apparent way out and my faith there dangling on the line. Naturally, my faith was the first thing to go before the wailing started. Funny thing though: with faith restored through prayer and counseling with my Christian friends and pastor, my life took dramatic changes. It was almost as though the Lord put me through lessons that strengthened my faith and then opened up doors to vistas I never even imagined!

But your walk through the wilderness right now is very real. And you are probably in a lot of pain, and under attack in the form of low self-esteem. But in fact, you are victorious! Don't let Satan bum you out. That's his job when you're down and out . . . don't give in to him. Instead begin to praise God for all your blessings. Praise Him for the testing and the strength. Praise Him for His faithfulness to you. In other words, begin to praise God for His promises and stop praying the problems. Let Him know that you know He's in charge and that He's going to bail you out! At times like these I cling to the Psalms . . . they are precious affirmations of all God's promises.

Your life is about to take on some dramatic changes. Hang on to your seat!

Dear Danuta:
Eleven years ago, I had an abortion. I was unmarried, had two children at the time, and the man I had an affair with insisted on the abortion.

I have not left my home in ten years. The doctors call it agoraphobia. I call it being a lost Christian.

I once read in the Bible that "no one, having put his hand to the plow, and looking back, is fit for the kingdom of God." It seems a lot more serious for me, a Christian, to have aborted a child, than if a non-Christian had done the same thing.

I've prayed so much that God has probably forgiven me. Yet I've lost the certainty that I once had of His love and acceptance. I've lost an innocence that can never be recaptured. But what about the "hand to the plow" thing? Is that judgment meant for people like me?

I can never forget that but for my decision, my child would have been with us. That is a message that might make other women view abortion differently. It is difficult to project into the future, but on this issue of abortion, you must. A decision made today will affect a woman's life forever—although I hope not as drastically as it has mine.

Dear Hand to the Plow:

You need to let go of the past.

You need to let go of sin.

You need to let go of guilt.

You even have to stop praying about this. Constantly asking for forgiveness only reinforces the suggestion that you don't have it.

Don't trust your emotions when it comes to spiritual matters. If you feel that you have lost God's love and acceptance, remember that that is *your* feeling, not His. Trust in the Word of God, not in your own feelings. Feelings and moods fluctuate. The love from the Lord abides forever.

And about the "hand to the plow" thing . . . that is describing someone who chooses to leave God. You're not one of them.

If you believe in Christ you must believe in your forgiveness, or else Christ died for nothing.

Dear Danuta:

I am thirty-four years old and was baptized when I was ten.

In college, I became disillusioned and turned away from church. I have committed many sins and paid dearly for them. God has punished me and has stripped me of everything and left me with nothing.

It's been a year now since I started watching your show, reading the Bible, and praying. It consumes me twenty-four hours a day. I have confessed my sins and asked God to forgive me and tell me what to do, but nothing ever happens—only silence.

What I want to know is this: Since the Bible says that God chooses whom He will be merciful to, are there some people whom He will continue to punish and never forgive? Is it too late for me to repent? I am afraid to move or think for fear that He will strike me dead. Everyone on your show receives instant peace and answers. But I don't.

Dear Afraid to Move:

If you are "afraid to move or think" for fear that He will strike you dead, then that fear is NOT from God. God is perfect love. The Bible says that perfect love casts out fear.

It is time to live . . . Christ said He came to give us life and life more abundantly.

"Living" means not being so obsessed by the Bible that you do not have time to exercise the Word in action.

If you are living in Christ, all God recognizes is the sweet perfume of Jesus covering you, not your sins. You must accept your salvation and LIVE in the light of it.

Know that God loves you. Get some sunshine and fresh air. Have fun . . . know joy, and you will see that Christ has been there all the time, waiting for you to accept your new life in Him.

God chooses to be merciful to those who call upon the name of

His dearly beloved Son who died for you. *You choose* whether to be covered by Christ or not. Satan is the only one who will never be forgiven—having known the glory of God and turning from that pure knowledge. Jesus died for all who call upon His name. It is *never* too late to say you're sorry. God is *merciful* and we are saved not through our good works but by *grace* through Christ Jesus.

And just to clear something up—everyone on the "700 Club" does not receive instant peace and answers. We humans are too obstinate in our nature for *instant* peace. God works on our weaknesses and over time we are able to see ourselves as He sees us. We are convicted of what we're doing wrong, make the appropriate changes, and then see the grace of God.

My suggestion to you—live! And rejoice!

———————

Why doesn't my loved one want to be saved?

Dear Danuta:

I am a new Christian and a new "700 Club" member. I'm making a genuine effort to live God's laws and apply them daily.

I pray every day for God to touch my husband's heart and bring him to Jesus. He is a bitter, cynical man who claims God has no place in his life. Our bleak financial status adds to my husband's cynicism, but I have hope that the Lord will answer my prayers.

Dear New Christian:

I am so glad you wrote to me. So often a new Christian is so eager for her spouse or loved ones to know Christ too that instead of drawing them to Him by their enthusiasm and oft expressed rewards, the opposite occurs—they are turned off.

Relax, don't press. Trust the Lord to save your husband. He will in His time. Meanwhile, avoid doing anything that will antagonize your husband against your newly found faith. Use wisdom. Study the Word; learn God's ways. Let His light shine through you. Let the fruit of the Spirit be developed in your life (Galatians 5:22); "Let patience have its perfect work, that you may be perfect and complete, lacking nothing" (James 1:4).

Have faith that the Lord will bring you and your husband together spiritually and that your prayers are heard. First Peter 3:1 speaks to wives in your position: "You wives be submissive to your own husbands, that even if some do not obey the word, they, without a word, may be won by the conduct of their wives."

I'm so happy that you have become a Christian and are earnestly working toward making a genuine effort to live for Him.

Dear Danuta:

My husband hates anyone and everything having to do with Christianity. I respect his wishes by not having anything to do with churches. It is hard to live with a man like this and I am sure it is hard for him to live with me. We love each other, but I lack fulfillment in this marriage because I cannot share the things that mean the most to me. My husband doesn't want me to go to church, so I don't. He doesn't like my Christian friends, so I don't associate with them. He doesn't want me to go to Bible study, so I don't. I am trying to pursue my faith alone by praying and reading the Bible. But it hurts not to find any other way to serve the Lord. I need God and I am sure that He is doing His best to strengthen this marriage.

Dear Needing God:

I have read your letter several times over and I want to be very careful in how I respond to it.

You say you are pursuing the Lord and you need Him and that He is with you and is strengthening you in your relationship with your husband. But, you also seem to be lacking fulfillment with your husband. May I suggest that the fulfillment you're lacking is not the fulfillment with your husband but rather your fulfillment with the Lord Jesus Christ. Your priorities are not set right.

To choose the wishes of your unsaved husband over the wishes of God Himself is incorrect. You say that you respect your husband's wishes and don't go to church or get involved with any Christian fellowship. Then, you go on to say that it really hurts that you can't serve the Lord in some way other than in prayer and reading the Word. Well, of course, it hurts. It hurts because you are not obeying God's law.

There is something you can do. You can pursue the Lord with all your heart. Go to church. Pray with others. Find fellowship. Your husband will be saved through you. But you have to start acting like you love the Lord. You have to start walking with Him. How would you expect the Lord to come to your rescue or to serve you with financial prosperity unless you first serve Him through acting on His Word.

Give yourself to Him. That's what you can do. Give yourself to Him, then watch what happens.

Dear Danuta:

I've fallen hard for a man—he's a hard worker and fun to be with. I know he is one with whom I would love to spend the rest of my life. I am fifty-four; he is fifty-seven.

He told me he loved me and there was talk of a ring. Then suddenly he started to change. He hasn't called in a week. He comes from a Christian background but hasn't attended services. He did say he wanted to start going to church on Sundays. But He has gone back on everything he spoke of doing with and for me. I'm not sure if I'm playing the part of the fool to wait for him to change.

Dear Not Sure:

The Lord uses the circumstances of our lives to teach and draw us nearer to Him. All kinds of lessons in patience, gentleness, humility take place as we learn to wait upon the Lord. He is faithful. We are to be full of faith too. Total trust in Him lifts us up and frees us from anxiety. Study Proverbs 3:5–7. Also in considering marriage, study 2 Corinthians 6:14 and Matthew 6:33.

Allow the Lord time to work things out for you. Make Psalms 37:3–5 very real in your life. Soon, your faith will shine forth as an example to others, including the man you are interested in marrying. If he is not a committed Christian, you should avoid marriage until he has given his life over to Christ.

Sometimes men need some "space" to work things out, especially as a relationship becomes serious. Don't panic if he hasn't called you in a week. Let him miss you. Let him think about you. Let him weigh you against the others. Your best tactic at times like these is silence, for several reasons. First, to let God work. If this man is for you by God's intention, he will have to learn to walk according to God's law. That may take a little time. Second, if this man is for you he must know it within himself without pushing from you. Keep silent.

But again, let me warn you, I receive many letters from women who are suffering because they live with unsaved husbands. Wait on God—He knows what He's doing!

———

How do I tithe
when I have no money?

Dear Danuta:

I feel very strongly the importance of tithing. But my family needs my paycheck and my parents are against taking such a big chunk of money that could go to help out for food.

I want to obey my parents. But I also want to uphold what is right with God.

Dear Waiting to Tithe:

Thank you so much for your letter. I can understand the concern that you might have in the area of tithing. On the one hand, you feel compelled to uphold the Word of God. On the other hand, you feel compelled to obey your parents. I cannot make that decision for you.

If money is a dividing factor in the harmony of your home, especially in terms of the relationship with your parents, then perhaps your tithing could be something other than money. Why not tithe 10 percent of your effort into helping others? Why not spend some time in service to those who need your help? In serving others, you serve God and it doesn't have to be with money. It can be with your heart. Your heart is good and your heart is generous; your intent is sincere. God will honor your efforts to Him.

Part 4

"I feel as if
I know you . . ."

Why do you "click" with me?

There are a lot of personal questions—about my background, how I was led to the Lord Jesus, how I met and married my husband, Kai, how I came to CBN, and who my family is. Funny questions. Controversial questions. And sometimes a brainstorm someone is itching to share.

My Friend, My Loving Sister in Christ:
I don't know why I like you, but there's something in you that "clicks" with me. When you laugh, your laughter is so contagious that I end up chuckling with you. Like the time you went fishing and caught a fish with a piece of cheese. That was really something!

I'm just sort of curious and want to know more about you.

Dear Curious:
You said in your letter you don't know why you like me, but that there's something that "clicks." I've got to say that click is Jesus.

Dear Danuta:
I am an avid viewer of your show and want you to know how much I appreciate your being a co-host on the "700 Club." I pray

for you and for the others in your ministry. I'd like to know a little more about you, especially your testimony about how you came to know Jesus. I bet it's a fascinating story.

Dear Avid Viewer:

Thank you for your interest in the "700 Club" and in my testimony. I would be glad to share it with you. I had always been interested in philosophy and later in school majored in the subject. So I was always looking for truth. Several years ago, I started a small philosophy group. We would meet each week to discuss various books and philosophers and swap books. Then we would reach each other's interpretations of them. One day I brought Nietzsche's book *The Anti-Christ* to the table and a friend of mine brought C. S. Lewis's *Mere Christianity.* After comparing both books, it dawned on us that Nietzsche was trying to defend his stand of nonbelief to such an extent that we saw him gradually becoming insane in his arguments. What was he fighting so strongly to deny? That's when we turned to *Mere Christianity* by C. S. Lewis.

Lewis had an argument that said you either choose the Lord or the devil; there is no in-between. Sooner or later you must face that decision. He also had an argument for the soul which was very interesting and an argument for the concept of eternity. We bantered for weeks on end about all these ideas.

Then, my future husband-to-be (at the time my best friend, Kai) suggested that I meet a man he had met five years before. His name was Reverend Harald Bredesen. Harald Bredesen explained in detail one night all the questions I had ever had about Christianity. I pounded him with questions that only a journalist could devise.

Halfway through my questions, I heard a voice say to me, "Your questions are not important!" It made me pause. I began to think that all my questions did not have to be answered in order for me to accept Christ into my life.

Then Harald reached over the table and said, "Do you want to accept Christ in your life tonight?"

Without hesitation, I said, "Yes." And so did my other two friends!

The philosophy group now became a Bible study group. We found a church; we studied the Bible and we grew very, very fast in the knowledge of the Lord.

Two years later, after coincidences and circumstances that only God could have put together, I found myself at CBN co-hosting the "700 Club." Ah, the subtlety of God's will!

A few months after leaving California and arriving in Virginia Beach, Kai, the man who first introduced me to Harald Bredesen, and I were married. It has been a whirlwind for me since meeting the Lord, and every time I turn the bend or go around the corner, He has another surprise for me. Life has not been dull! And all those other things that I was searching for, I have found in the Lord Jesus Christ.

I can hardly wait to see what else He has in store for me! He has already shown me the path of life and the fullness of joy (Psalms 16:11).

Dear Danuta:

Occasionally you've talked about your father on the show. I'm really interested in him and your background. Can you tell me more?

Dear Interested:

Everyone thinks their family is unique. I guess mine is, but we also share many of the struggles that first-generation Americans face.

After I was born in England, my family emigrated to the

United States. My father was a Polish war hero who escaped three times from the Germans during World War II. My mother is an English nurse.

We moved around a lot when we came to America. My father was a sculptor and a ski instructor. So in winter he taught skiing and in the summer he was an artist. By the time I was eighteen, my brothers and I had gone to fifteen different schools. I never was in one place long enough to make lasting friends. Once we lived in a tent which a priest had talked a circus into donating for us. And once we ate venison for several months, but not because my father was a hunter. He would try to hunt with a bow and arrow, but he was too softhearted to shoot anything! We had meat because a neighbor hit a deer with his truck!

Looking back on my childhood, I hardly feel deprived. It was great! Maybe because we were always encouraged to do things, I learned very early to take advantage of my talents and opportunities. We learned the value of love above material possessions. We learned what was important to *life* and what was not!

I learned to ski at the age of three and was on the ski patrol when I was only eight years old. That made me one of the youngest, if not the youngest, member of the ski patrol in the United States!

And when I was in college in California, I developed a technique for teaching babies how to swim. That helped me pay for college and also gave me the opportunity to write my first book, *Waterproof Your Baby in One Week.*

Dear Danuta:
I'm hoping to pursue a career in Christian broadcasting. What I want to know is whether you always knew you wanted to be in television. How did you start your career?

Dear Hoping for a Career:

I must say that I knew I wanted to do something meaningful, even when I was very young. I may not have known exactly where God would lead me, but I did know that God had given me an unknown destiny—it was my job to discover my talents.

When I was a high school senior, my family was living in Anchorage, Alaska. The owner of the local television station was encouraging high school students to take an interest in broadcasting. So he started a program called "The Varsity Show" on Saturday afternoons. It was run entirely by high schoolers, and one of them was me.

That show changed my life. I became the "Dick Clark of Anchorage"! I played records on the show and talked about music. I also learned about television, on and off camera. One of my jobs was going to the airport every evening to pick up the "Huntley-Brinkley Report" which was flown in from Seattle. If the tape didn't come in on time, there was no news.

Before that, I was going to be an oceanographer or a pediatrician. But the first time I walked into the television studio, I knew I wanted to be a communicator! But it was a long haul.

When I went to college, I took as many courses as I could in journalism and in philosophy, my other great love. My degree is in communications from the University of Colorado. But my interest in philosophy is deep, too. In fact, it eventually led me to commit myself to Christ and to a study of God's Word. My entry into broadcasting didn't happen overnight. I worked as a camera operator at KTAR-TV in Phoenix, a ski reporter for a radio news bureau in San Francisco, a radio reporter and anchor in San Diego, a morning talk-show hostess for KFMB in San Diego, a disc jockey for a radio station, a news director, and finally, co-host of the "700 Club" at CBN. Now at CBN, I've been able to combine my skill at broadcasting with my knowledge of the Word. And I'm also expanding my career as a Christian communicator into other areas. I'm excited about my next writing project—a book which will center on the question "Searching for God." So many Christians talk about joy, but they don't act joyful. They talk about freedom, but they don't act free! These things are scaring nonbelievers off. My next book is going to shake some peaches from the tree! My best advice is to get a good education, and start in a small market doing small things; grow from there.

Dear Danuta:

My wife and I are a couple of your fans who see you often on the "700 Club." You add such a sparkle to the show. We love you because God is seen so very much in you.

You look as though you're having so much fun on the show. How did God lead you to become part of the "700 Club?"

Dear Couple of Fans:

You asked what led me to Christian TV. I'm doing what I do only because God had a plan for me and I was available and willing to follow Him.

I had no idea my life would change until God brought about a series of incredible miracles in my life. The first one was when my co-host on the "Sun Up San Diego" show, Jerry G. Bishop, told me about a dream he had. He said he never remembers his dreams, but this time he did. He dreamed he saw me on national TV interviewing world leaders for Jesus Christ.

I had become a Christian a few months before, but I didn't believe Jerry. "You're out of your mind," I told him.

At that time, I was sure my next stop was a bigger network show, maybe in Los Angeles or New York. I had been talking to a producer about co-hosting a show called "Hour Magazine." Besides, the co-hosts who preceded me at KFMB in San Diego were

Raquel Welch and Sarah Purcell—I figured I would just follow in their footsteps.

The second miracle happened three days later when a woman I'd never seen before came up to me when I was lying on the beach. The woman said, "Hi! You don't know me, but I know you. My husband had a dream about you. He dreamed that he and our son were climbing up these long, steep stairs to see a great rabbi at the top. When they got to the top, you were standing there."

What did it all mean? I sure didn't know.

The next day, when Reverend Harald Bredesen, the man who led me to the Lord, phoned me, I told him about these two strange dreams. He insisted that I send a resumé and a videotape to the Christian Broadcasting Network and tell them about the two experiences.

Well, I did. And I didn't hear a thing from CBN for nine months! By that time, I'd forgotten all about CBN.

Then one day, I got a message that Michael Little from CBN had phoned. He called me again that night at home to tell me someone had found my tape and letter in a drawer after cleaning out a desk. No one had seen the tape or letter until then!

He also said, "We've been loooking for someone like you for a long time."

Things happened so fast after that. Two weeks later—on my birthday—I quit both my jobs on San Diego TV and radio, packed my cat and my African violets, and drove clear across the country to do only God knew what!

I started out as foreign correspondent. But soon I was co-hosting the show with Pat Robertson and Ben Kinchlow. And we've been a team ever since. Besides working together on camera, we review all the taped features, we screen all the guests, and we pray together—every single workday.

And that wasn't the last miracle. Six months after I got to Virginia Beach, I married Kai Soderman, my best friend for the past seven years.

Something heavenly compelled me to take these steps. Through it all, I've learned not to ask questions but to trust Him and not hold on too tightly to anything else but Him. Whatever He wants, I'll do!

———————

What *can* women do?

Dear Danuta:

As a young woman, I am troubled by the attitude that a "good Christian woman should always be at home."

You strike me as an independent, forceful woman. Really, how do you feel about the choices Christian women are faced with nowadays? What *can* Christian women do?

Dear Troubled:

A better question might be, what CAN'T a Christian woman do? We have the power to change our nation and our world toward a more godly expression of life. We have the power to raise our children according to godly principles. We have the power to invest our time in politics, and encourage our Christian leaders in government.

We have the power to be anything we want to be. We have the ability to go to any school and study any discipline or trade. The Bible teaches us perseverance. With that and the will of God, anything is possible!

As women we are not only capable of being the best we can be, but as Christians, we are obligated! We are to live life MORE abundantly, to be the head and not the tail.

Children do need a mother. But even in the home we are capable of growing. If you haven't finished college or high school, you can take correspondence courses. You can try your hand at writing magazine articles, letters to the editor, art classes, learning a foreign language . . . the list is endless.

The idea that the "little woman" has to sit at home with no mind of her own and no interests outside the home is not only unhealthy, it's inhuman! We have minds that need to be stimulated; we need to cultivate interests in our community and the world around us. We are co-heirs of the grace of life (1 Peter 3:7) with men, and we must assume our share of the responsibilities in life.

Many Christian women think the ideal is to be a beautiful violet wilting on the wallpaper, with no opinions, no personal power, and no active intelligence; somehow, we must submit our humanness to the male of the species. Nothing could be further from the truth. Jesus died to take away our sins, not to take away our minds!

Christian women have enormous responsibilities to add to our society a moral conscience through our children, our businesses, and our homes; if we are married, to support and nurture our husbands; as citizens, to add our voice to the moral conscience of our nation; to add beauty and character to our world; and to pray.

All things are possible in Christ. I have been a race-car driver, a ski instructor, a swim instructor, a scuba diver, a sky diver, a student, a social activist, a writer, a poet, a painter, a woman, and a wife, and there is so much more to become!

Will my pet go to heaven?

Dear Danuta:

With your devotion to the Lord and love for God's critters, I could think of no one better able to answer this question: Is there a puppy dog heaven?

Dear Critter Lover:

In response to your question—I hope so, though the Bible doesn't say anything about a heaven for animals. If heaven is all that we hope it to be, my pets may be there, but when I am in the presence of God I doubt I will miss them in the face of the Creator of all things.

Dear Danuta:

I have a question which I have never had a good answer to. When I ask it, I get several responses:

1. *Who cares?*
2. *When the Rapture happens, we won't care.*
3. *Don't worry about foolish things.*

Out of curiosity, could you tell me what will happen to our pets and animals during and after the Rapture? Will my cat and dog in the house, my horse in the stall, etc., starve to death because my whole family will be gone?

Dear After the Rapture:

Do you really believe that God would let your animals starve? After all, they are part of His creation, too.

No one knows what will happen before, during, and after the Rapture, and it would be pure speculation to deal with that question.

I would hope that just as Jesus has made plans for me, He has also made plans for all His creation. The Bible tells us not a sparrow will fall from the sky that God does not know about. And we are told that when Christ returns and peace reigns upon the earth, the lion and the lamb will lie together in peace. God's creation will continue!

———

Here's a great idea!

Dear Danuta:

I am writing to ask your advice.

Before I became a Christian, I used to go out to my favorite nightclub where my boyfriend was a singer. I no longer go to any lounges, but I find I miss the atmosphere of meeting friends at a quaint candlelit table and listening to music.

For the past few years since giving my life to the Lord, I think He has been calling me to get something similar started for Christians—with Christian singing groups or comedians, and pizza instead of liquor. I feel this would be a great opportunity for Christians to go out and have fun or bring their not-yet-Christian friends to introduce them to a better way.

I do not have a lot of money saved up, but I do know that if it is God's idea, He can provide the means. I'm asking your advice because I respect your opinion, and I think you might understand what I'm trying to do. Am I out of line? Do you think my idea of a Christian lounge is too close to worldliness?

Dear Great Opportunity:

I think your idea of a Christian nightclub is a fantastic one. We are told to go out into the world and spread the good news, and that's a terrific way of doing it!

Christians need to unwind, just like other people. There's nothing wrong with candlelight, pizza, and having a good time. It is so desperately needed. Go for it!

Part 5

"If you're ever
in Des Moines . . ."

I love that peach dress!

Then there are unabashed fans who just write to let me know that they relate to something they like about me. They have their own ideas about my makeup, my wardrobe, the colors I wear, my hairdo . . . and everybody has an opinion!

Dear Danuta:

As one on a limited budget, I seldom am able to buy new clothes. I am very appreciative of the stylish and fashionable manner in which you mix and match your wardrobe pieces. I don't think I've ever seen Jane Pauley wear the same outfit twice—how unrealistic.

Dear Danuta:

Can't you do something with your hair? A more stylish hairdo would be so becoming.

Dear Danuta:

I love your hair. You are able to wear it so many different ways and have it still look nice.

Dear Danuta:

You look wonderful in that peach dress.

Dear Danuta:

Have you ever been color coordinated? You should never wear orange or yellow or peach!

Dear Danuta:

You look terrific in yellow and orange.

Dear Danuta:

I am amazed how your clothes remain preserved for so long. You look really super nice on TV with the way you match your clothes.

Dear Danuta:

How do you launder your clothing?

Dear Danuta:

Your nails are short, but they are nice and that is fashionable, really. I get all cheerful when I watch you on TV 'cause you truly are a sample of a real Christian lady for the Lord.

Dear Danuta:

No one can ever say you spend too much time beautifying yourself for the world.

Dear Danuta:

What size dress do you wear?

Dear Danuta:

You seem to be putting on some weight. I'd like to tell you about Herbalife.

Dear Polish Princess:

I want to compliment you on the way you dress. I hope you never put on any more makeup and jewelry.

Dear Danuta:

Why don't you wear clothes that look more professional? A business suit that is in style—dress more like Jane Pauley.

Dear Danuta:

I appreciate the fact that you are willing to be seen wearing the same clothes over and over. It is so foolish to have on a different outfit for every show, which is the manner in which Jane Pauley dresses.

Dear Concerned Readers:

Even Jane Pauley has a budget for clothes, and even she has worn the same outfit more than once. At some television stations the hosts of TV shows are given clothes to wear for a day or to advertise a store. (The TV people do not keep the clothes, in most cases.)

At CBN we do not promote clothing stores for free outfits and we must be good stewards of the donations from our partners, so we do not spend lavish amounts of money on our clothes. At the same time, I try to wear outfits that coordinate with other items in my wardrobe to stretch the variety of my choices.

While I concentrate on a professionl appearance, I am not so concerned about how many clothes I have. There are many more important things to deal with, such as hunger, poverty, and despair in the world.

About that blonde . . .

Dear Pat Robertson:

Just want to write and tell you that blonde sure MINISTERS just by being enthusiastic, pleasant, nice looking, and interested in her work.

She doesn't just do a job . . . she "ministers."

I felt it deserved a postage stamp just to tell you so.

Dear Danuta:

Today is your birthday, and since I am a firm believer in giving out roses while people can still smell them, I think your birthday is a good time to tell you what a blessing you are to me and countless others.

Maybe I'm just a fanciful old lady—I don't feel old, although my driver's license says I'm seventy-six—but in thinking of you and your effervescent joy in the Lord, I began thinking of the 139th Psalm and of God's plan for your life long ago. I could almost see Him putting together all the qualities that would make up the personality of this lovely little blue-eyed child that was to be. I think He must have smiled—don't you?

He might have even said, "This child is going to love life and will go many places and see and do many things, all of which will prepare her for the day when she will commit herself to My service. Then I will show her how she can bless others for My sake. Many will come to know Me; many will be healed; many will be blessed!" Then I think He smiled again.

I think my loving Father is more than satisfied that His long-ago plans for a little blue-eyed Polish girl have all come to pass so far, and will culminate someday when He smiles again and welcomes her Home.

God bless you again, honey—you sure have blessed me.

Dear Danuta:

This is part of your fan mail to tell you how much my husband and I appreciate you on the "700 Club."

There's a freshness about you that's so delightful. Longtime Christians in media are so often staid, reserved, and kind of stuffy. (Since I'm a longtime Christian, I'm talking about my own crowd.) You are none of these things. Yet your love for God is clear and unmistakable.

I would really love to meet you someday to hear about your life and what your thoughts are about Christian media.

If you ever come to Des Moines and need a place to stay, please give me a call.

Dear Danuta:

You are to be commended on your fine interview of Captain John Testrake [pilot of hijacked airplane]. You ask pertinent questions and do not interrupt.

The secular media could learn a lot from watching the "700 Club."

P.S. Tell Pat to give you a raise! You put Jane Pauley to shame!

Dear Danuta:

I just got through watching the "700 Club" and I decided to write to tell you how much I enjoy you on the program.

I am a practicing Catholic but I still enjoy watching your program. You have a lot of very interesting subjects. It's a great show and most of it, I feel, is because you're on it.

You're very intelligent and a great interviewer, not to take anything away from Pat and Ben. Also, you're a lot prettier than they are. I love your smile. You've got a God-given talent and beauty and that makes you a very special lady.

This is starting to sound like a fan letter, isn't it? In a way, I guess it is.

Dear Danuta:

I wanted to let you know that I appreciate the questions you ask Pat when he is explaining reasons for what God does or does not do.

Most television programs do not address obvious questions that arise during these explanations. I think this is one of the reasons that unsaved people, like my husband, are critical of Christians and Christian programs. Sometimes when I'm watching the "700 Club," these obvious questions pop into my head. I know my husband is thinking the same thing. Then you will suddenly ask Pat that same question.

Pat will look at you with an expression that says, "What are you trying to do to me?" So it is obvious that you two have not rehearsed it. And Pat will come up with what is usually a satisfactory answer. I know this gives credibility to your program in my husband's eyes.

So keep on asking those questions, Danuta. I really enjoy seeing that look on Pat's face.

Dear Danuta:

Me and my wife wanted to write and encourage you. We think you're precious. We're a couple of your fans who see you often on the "700 Club."

You make the show a delight. Especially today, this Wednesday, the 31st of July. I just felt like you needed some love and attention, some encouragement.

Your personality isn't like anyone else's. It's unique. Usually unexpected things come out of you. And it blesses me. We wanted you to know that God is seen so very much in your childlikeness. God is like a child. He makes things simple. And so we love you.

But even if you weren't precious, we'd love you because we're not looking for you to entertain us. So you can relax and be precious. Thanks for letting God be in you. Wish you were here. We'd give you a hug.

P.S. I accidentally got spaghetti sauce on the top left. It's delicious.

Dear Delicious:

Wow! And boy am I encouraged. Your adorable and precious letter made my day—maybe my whole week. I'm sure I don't deserve all those plaudits, but thanks for taking the time to express your love. I deeply appreciate it.

Blessings to you both as you go about encouraging.

Yummy spaghetti.

The cat who didn't choose MTV

Dear Danuta:

I must write to you this once more. I wrote to you a couple of weeks ago to say how I appreciated the role you fill on the "700 Club." But I didn't tell you my little story. And since, in a way, you are responsible, I would like to.

For years and years, I had a preconceived notion of Christians—Southern-accented men who yelled on radio and TV during Sunday-morning hours. I couldn't change stations fast enough. "Ignorance," I thought (in my own ignorance).

One evening while watching cable TV, my cat stepped on the remote control unit, changing the channel. Suddenly you came on doing an interview. I couldn't pigeonhole what I was watching until the talk turned to God. But you weren't yelling and didn't use improper grammar and this wasn't early Sunday morning!

The rest of the program held my attention, too.

I watched the next night and the next. I even prayed with you over the next couple of weeks and started reading the New Testament. Then I called your toll-free number for advice on a church to attend. I wanted one with life, one where the Holy Spirit was working. The woman I talked to recommended an Assembly of God church. I didn't know what that was, but I found one here, and much to my amazement, it was just what I was looking for. I have since joined.

The point of this letter, Danuta, isn't to say "the cat stepped on my remote control unit one night" but to say that God has changed my heart. My judgments, reactions, priorities, and attitudes have all changed.

If there had been no CBN (if, say, the cat had stepped on MTV), I would still be where I used to be.

P.S. Don't bother answering this. My cat Toby says "hi."

Dear Toby's Owner:

What a precious and beautifully expressed testimony. Thank you so much for sharing it. And it is no bother to welcome a new member to the family of God.

Stay in the Word. Study—don't just read it. Pray often. Stay in fellowship. And most of all, don't look just to people for examples, but go back to Christ and His teachings to determine how He would have responded to a situation.

Blessings to you, and thanks so much for sharing your story.

Hi, Toby.

Out of the mouths
of babes . . .

Dear Danuta:

I'm eleven years old but I have a good idea.

If only the whole world could join hands, a chain could be formed all the way around the world. Maybe all of us could be friends. I'm a born-again Christian and I love God very much.

Dear Little Sister:

Yes, that really is a neat idea. And wouldn't it be wonderful if more and more people did have Christ in common? Then many problems between nations could be more easily solved and tensions would be eased, even on a local level. Let's keep praying for leaders here and abroad.

Your letter was an inspiration to me. Keep on loving God, for even a child is known by her (or his) actions. What you do is important and it is important that you remain near God throughout your teen years, never drifting away and wasting part of your life. Thanks for writing to share your ideas with me—you sound like a real sweetheart.

Dear Danuta:

With your devotion to the Lord and love for God's critters, I could think of no one better able to answer this question: Is there a puppy dog heaven?

Dear Danuta:

Recently my wife decided to leave our home. We both belong to a church, and she claims to be born-again, but I feel she fell prey to the temptations of the world. How else could she claim to be a Christian and leave her children and husband like this?

Dear Danuta:

God is mad at me and He's turned away. And I'm wasting my time trying to change God's curse into a blessing. But I thought I'd make one last try. *You* pray for me. He's not listening to me. Maybe He'll listen to you.

Dear Danuta:

My son joined the Hare Krishna movement right after college and has been with these people almost ten years. Now he says he wants to come home to visit for a month or so. Please pray not only that my son will see the truth but that God will guide my husband and me as to how to deal with this visit.

Dear Danuta:

I am in love with Jim, but he is taking so long in deciding to marry me. Please pray that the Lord will make Jim love me and show us the way to a marriage. Please pray too that this will be a good marriage.